Workplace Violence

A Continuum from Threat to Death

Mittie D. Southerland, Ph.D.
Murray State College

Pamela A. Collins, Ed.D., C.F.E.
Eastern Kentucky University

Kathryn E. Scarborough, Ph.D.
Eastern Kentucky University

anderson publishing co.
2035 Reading Rd.
Cincinnati, OH 45202
1-800-582-7295

Workplace Violence: A Continuum from Threat to Death

Copyright © 1997 Anderson Publishing Co.
2035 Reading Rd.
Cincinnati, OH 45202

Phone 800.582.7295 or 513.421.4142
Web Site www.andersonpublishing.com

ISBN 0-87084-895-X
Library of Congress Catalog Number 97-72953

EDITOR Gail Eccleston
ASSISTANT EDITOR Elizabeth A. Shipp
ACQUISITIONS EDITOR Michael C. Braswell

Acknowledgments

A text based on original research comes together only after much sacrifice by those close to the authors. Our families, colleagues, and students gave us much needed encouragement, support, and tolerance. Ms. June Carver and her staff, NASA-UKTAC, University of Kentucky, provided vital assistance in the "search" for our data.

We appreciate the excellent editorial support we received from the Anderson Publishing Co. team. Kelly Grondin, Director, Criminal Justice/Paralegal Division, and Gail Eccleston, Editor, are true professionals. We owe them much for their patience, support, and editorial assistance. Bill Simon and Michael Braswell demonstrated their faith in this project, and for that we are most grateful. We are also indebted to the reviewers whose comments assisted us greatly in refining the text.

Southerland especially thanks and dedicates her efforts to her companion, friend, and husband, Joel, and to her daughters, Rachel and Harper, who have endured the countless hours she has spent away from them while reading, coding, and writing. They keep her life interesting. Southerland owes much to her research assistants, Darryl Barnes and Bridgette West, and her students at Murray State University, who assisted with the organization and then collection of various parts of the data.

Collins is forever indebted to her parents, Seba and Ernest Collins, for their support and encouragement throughout the years and their belief in the lifelong pursuit of knowledge.

Scarborough has much gratitude to her grandfather, the late J.M. Scarborough, who believed in her by his consistent support through her college years, to her mother, Nan Miller, who taught her the joy of the written word, and to Cheryl Gentry who introduced her to Harper Lee and Scout. Finally to K.C., the raison d'être.

We dedicate this book to the victims of workplace violence and to the employers who strive to prevent violence in their workplaces.

Preface

May 17, 1995—James Floyd Davis, after being fired from an Asheville, North Carolina, tool company, returned for the last time. It wasn't his paycheck that he was after; he came armed with an M-1 rifle and a semi-automatic handgun. When he had finished his rampage, he left three co-workers dead and injured a fourth.

Davis surrendered to police without incident and was led in handcuffs from the facility. According to employees, this did not come as a surprise. Davis was described by co-workers as a "dangerous and paranoid man." He was said to have a firing range in his basement and often brought weapons to work to show them off to other employees.

Davis had received numerous warnings for several years against fighting with his fellow employees. These complaints and warnings continued until the company finally took action and fired him. Although company officials would not comment on what the final incident was that resulted in his termination, it is known that on that fateful Wednesday morning, Davis purchased an M-1 rifle at a pawn shop and arrived at the plant at 11:30 a.m. to begin his killing spree.

The *Davis* case is similar to many others that provide the impetus for this text. The circumstances in his case were somewhat unusual because of his choice of weapon. Yet the incident reminds us of too many similar incidents we have studied.

Just when we suppose we have seen every type of workplace violence that exists, a new twist occurs. The next case is atypical because of the site, location, motivation, and amount of warning given to the employer, but the killing is all too familiar. It was 5 a.m. Friday, February 9, 1996. The location was a small blue and white municipal trailer that served as headquarters for the cleanup detail for Ft. Lauderdale, Florida, parks and beaches. The trailer was located a few yards back from the palm-fringed Intracoastal Waterway separating Ft. Lauderdale Beach from the mainland.

Exactly 14 months before the incident, Clifton McCree, 41, had been fired for testing positive for drugs, threatening and harassing co-workers, and being rude to the public. He vowed revenge, and February 9 was the day he chose to take that revenge.

McCree barged into the trailer where he had once worked and said "All of you . . . are going to die." He opened fire with a 9mm handgun, reloading once. The sole survivor of the incident turned and ran to the door. A bullet flew past her as she escaped unharmed. Five workers were killed and a sixth was critically wounded as they sat at a conference table receiving their daily assignments for litter removal. All six of the killed and injured were white males between 36 and 46 years of age.

At least 14 shots were fired before McCree used the gun to kill himself. He never touched the pistol that was in the shoulder holster under his jacket. McCree carried a suicide note.

Police received a 911 call from the critically wounded man who called from a telephone in the trailer. The victims were found by a second crew who reported for work at 6 a.m.

The alleged motivation in this incident makes it unique. Our research reflected no similar motivation. Survivors of this incident claimed that the motivation was racial, not hatred of his former boss or the agency. McCree was black. One survivor said that McCree had had a grudge against all white people. A niece of the critically wounded man said McCree had once stated that white people shouldn't be able to live. According to the niece, her uncle had repeatedly told officials that McCree was dangerous. This man also told his sister to sue the city if he didn't survive his injury because he had been telling them for a year and a half that McCree was going to do something like this. Other co-workers remembered McCree threatening revenge. One said that McCree constantly fought with co-workers and thought that everyone was out to get him (Frisaro, 1996).

Lethal violence is a subject that grasps the imagination. Its mystique heightens the inquisitive nature in most of us. This is apparent by the box office success of movies such as *Silence of the Lambs* and *Falling Down*. We want to know what causes someone to destroy the most precious commodity on earth, a life. Interest in the subject of violence in the workplace has grown since the early 1980s, stimulated primarily by incidents of mass murder in the workplace. Workers and employers want to know the clues that might predict such violence and the actions that can be taken to prevent it from happening to them or their organization.

Workplace violence has been examined from various perspectives ranging from simple assaults and sexual harassment to mass murder. It is important to note that, for purposes of this text, we have chosen to deal with incidents of workplace violence in which death did result or could have resulted. This is the type of workplace violence that strikes the most fear in our communities and nation of workers. We have also chosen to deal with the portion of the workplace violence phenomenon that has the greatest potential for preventive action, that is, violence committed by someone with a known link to the workplace in which the violence occurs. When the offender is known to the organizational members, there may be occasions in which *clues* of future violence will surface and preventive action may be taken. Additionally, these types of cases allow us to examine organizational behaviors that may contribute to the incidence of attempted and successful workplace "homicide." The fact that many organizations are not represented in the sites of workplace violence may give us clues for identifying a preventive organizational climate.

When we first began our empirical examination of the phenomenon in 1991, we were convinced that the form of workplace violence we call "lethal" was of vital importance to all workers. Our motivation for conducting the research and writing this book stemmed from the same basic human emotions most of us experience when we read about or are faced directly with an incident of violence in the workplace. We are at once repulsed that anyone could commit such a crime *and* we are intellectually stimulated to determine what happened, why it happened, and what can be done to prevent it from happening in the future.

Many researchers have sought to answer the *why* question as it pertains to lethal violence. Their research is presented in this text when relevant. Reference to additional readings are provided when appropriate. This text carves a different niche that empirically examines *lethal* and *potentially lethal* violence in the workplace and addresses the following questions:

- *Who* is the offender?
- *Who* is the victim?
- *What* happens?
- *When* does this type of violence take place?
- *Where* do these incidents occur?
- In *what* kinds of workplaces?
- *Why* does it happen?
- *How* does it occur?

Illustrative cases that represent the diverse nature of workplace violence incidents are presented in Chapter 3. Much of the prior literature on this topic, the discussion, and subsequent recommendations on workplace violence have been based on sensational cases such as the Clifton McCree case previously presented. However, this research paints a much broader picture of the problem and reveals the reality of workplace violence. The common scenario is very different than the sensational incidents that are easily recognized by the general public.

This text not only presents the findings of our research—which describe the incidents, offenders, and victims of workplace violence—but it offers recommendations for prevention, policy, and dealing with the aftermath of workplace violence. Additionally, several opportunities are available for you to "put the materials to work" in your workplace.

Mittie D. Southerland
Murray State University

Pamela A. Collins
Eastern Kentucky University

Kathryn E. Scarborough
Eastern Kentucky University

Table of Contents

1   Violence in the Workplace

Violence is an issue of great public interest. It is a serious social problem that has devastating effects on the quality of life and the economy within our communities. Academicians in the field of criminal justice, criminology, sociology, psychology, and public health have devoted much attention to this problem in recent years. An upsurge of violent behavior, which had not been experienced in the United States since the early 1930s, began in the late 1970s and peaked in 1980. A new upward trend began again in 1988 and had its first reduction in 1994. The number of persons murdered in the United States in 1994 was estimated at 23,305, resulting in a rate of 9 per 100,000 inhabitants. The murder rate for 1994 was 4 percent lower than in 1990, but 14 percent above the 1985 rate (U.S. Department of Justice, 1995). The rate declined in 1995 to an estimated 21,597 murders. The rate was slightly lower than in 1994 at 8.2 per 100,000 (U.S. Department of Justice, 1996).

Violence in the workplace has been described as a public health problem of significant proportion. In 1984, Surgeon General C. Everett Koop declared that "violence in American public and private life has indeed assumed the proportion of an epidemic" (National Committee for Injury, 1989).

The extent of violence in the American workplace often depends upon how the "workplace" is defined and what kinds of crimes are included in the definition. Occupational Violent Crime (OVC) is defined as, "intentional battery, rape, or homicide during the course of employment" (Hales, Seligman, Newman & Timbrook, 1988). The difficulty in measuring the complete impact of OVC is that there is no uniform data source. This fact leads to many misperceptions of the nature and problem of violent crime in the workplace. For example, many people have the perception that the risk of OVC for postal workers is much higher than most other professions, resulting in the phrase "going postal," which has become synonymous with workplace violence. In reality, the risk of death for postal workers in the workplace is much lower than media reports about post office shootings would suggest. In fact, the risk of death for the U.S. Postal Service's 892,000 employees is 2.5 times *lower* than that of all workers nationwide (CDC, 1992). One might question where this misperception originates. Is it a result of overconcentrated media attention, or some other form of misdirection? In a 1963 essay, C. Wright Mills mused about the relative effect of mass media and person-to-person communication on public opinion. He concluded that, "The American public is neither a sandheap of individuals each making up his own mind, nor a regimented mass manipulated by monopolized media of communication" (Mills, 1972:184). From Mills' perspective the misperception is due to a combination of both mass media and person-to-person communication.

History

Workplace violence is not a new phenomenon; it is as old as the relationship between employer and employee. It was not until the 1980s, however, that workplace violence became recognized nationally when a United States postal worker, Patrick Sherill, killed 14 people and wounded six in a violent rampage. This case was instrumental in the labeling and defining of workplace violence as an Occupational Violent Crime because it was one of the first cases of workplace violence involving the murder or attempted murder of such a large number of people in a single incident.

A wave of shootings by postal employees over the decade that followed the Sherill incident has resulted in 34 deaths and approximately 2,000 cases of postal worker "assaults," which include verbal threats as well as physical attacks. These events have permanently scarred the agency. A backlash against the postal service prompted the agency to reconsider employee training and screening policies (*New York Times,* 1993:A19).

Another significant event in bringing workplace violence to the forefront was an article titled "Fatal Occupational Injuries," that appeared in the *Journal of the American Medical Association.* The article identified these injuries as a public health concern and challenged the Occupational Safety and Health Administration (OSHA) to develop standards requiring protection of workers from assaultive injury in the workplace (Baker, Samkoff, Fisher & Van Buren, 1982). Dietz and Baker (1987) concluded that the primary result of the OVC research conducted in the mid 1980s was a heightened awareness that OSHA's failure to give attention to homicide in the workplace reflected the belief that homicide is a criminal justice problem, not a health and safety problem. They recommended that administrative rule-makers in regulatory agencies such as OSHA should be involved in both the *preventive* and *remedial* aspects of workplace violence.

It was not until a study by the National Institute of Occupational Safety Health (NIOSH), was released in 1993 that a greater understanding developed regarding the magnitude of the problem and its far-reaching implications to America's workforce. Although there has been a proliferation of scholarship on violence in the workplace in the last few years, much of this discussion has been based upon two primary data sources: the NIOSH study and the United States Bureau of Labor Statistics. Aside from these two sources, very little information is available on this subject for the United States. These two data sources alone do not accurately portray the nature and extent of OVC in the workplace.

Scope of the Problem

There have been a number of studies conducted in the last few years to assess the extent of workplace violence. Although the results differ somewhat depending on the data source used, the results indicate that OVC is a workplace safety issue that needs attention.

"Homicide is the leading cause of on-the-job death for workers in New York City," according to the Federal Bureau of Labor Statistics. In 1991, 177 people died as a result of injuries sustained while they were working in New York and 69 percent of these deaths were homicides. The workers' homicide rate is particularly high in New York City; statistics from 32 states indicate that in the nation as a whole only 14 percent of workplace death were homicides. However, a direct comparison of the two figures may be deceptive because the Bureau of Labor Statistics has not completed other homicide rate studies for other major U.S. cities and the 14 percent cited for the entire nation takes into account a combination of rural, urban, and suburban work sites (*New York Times*, 1993:B1).

Although it would be difficult to estimate the cost of these incidents to businesses, especially with regard to the loss of human life, it is possible to estimate other financial losses for the company. The Safe Workplace Institute has estimated that the annual cost of occupational violence to American businesses is approximately $4.2 billion. The Institute found that there were 11,000 serious incidents that cost employers $250,000 each; 30,000 medium-severity incidents with a $25,000 price tag per incident; and 70,000 lower-severity incidents with a cost to employers of $10,000 per occurrence, totaling $4.2 billion. These financial losses were calculated based upon losses in productivity, employee turnover and associated costs, litigation and legal fees (Kadaba, 1993:F1).

A number of studies have sought to define the scope of workplace violence but the most comprehensive and widely cited study was undertaken by the National Institute for Occupational Safety and Health (NIOSH), Division of Safety Research. This study was conducted from 1980-1989 and utilized both demographic and injury event information from state death certificates to examine United States fatal occupational injuries, including homicides. NIOSH used information taken from the National Traumatic Surveillance Data which contains death certificates, reported by each state's office of vital statistics, that meet the following criteria:

1. age at death—16 or older;

2. positive response to the "injury"-at-work item; and

3. having an external cause of death.

NIOSH chose to use death certificates as the source of information because they are available for all workers who are killed, regardless of their employment characteristics. Unlike Workers Compensation Claims and Occupational Safety and Health Administration (OSHA) Fatality Files, death certificate data are not limited by state of residence, occupation, industry, size of firm, or other employment characteristics. Death certificates contain information on the type of fatal injury and on demographic characteristics of killed workers. Moreover, these data are standardized throughout the United States. These data incorporate *all* occupational fatalities, including nonviolent incidents (e.g., automobile or other types of accidents) and homicides; however, we have chosen to present only the NIOSH information on homicide. According to the NIOSH study, homicides accounted for approximately 12 percent of all work-related deaths. This amounts to about 7,631 homicides out of 63,589 workplace deaths (NIOSH, 1993). Tables 1.1 and 1.2 summarize the NIOSH results of workplace death based upon workers by industry and occupation.

Table 1.1
Occupational Homicides by Industry

Occupational Homicide: Numbers and Rates per 100,000 Workers by Industry for a Ten (10) Year Period: NIOSH 1993		
Occupation	**Number**	**Rate**
Retail Trade	1,660	1.66
Public Administration	1,540	1.54
Transportation, Communication, Public Utility	1,470	1.47
Construction	650	0.65
Personal Services	610	0.61
Agriculture, Fisheries, Forestry	570	0.57
Mining	480	0.48
Finance, Insurance, Real Estate	390	0.39
Manufacturing	270	0.27
Wholesale Trade	190	0.19

Source: NIOSH (1993, August). *Fatal Injuries to Workers in the United States, 1980-1989: A Decade of Surveillance,* DHHS (NIOSH) No. 93-108, Cincinnati, OH.

Table 1.2
Occupational Homicides by Occupation

Occupational Homicides: Number and Rate per 100,000 Workers by Occupation for a Ten (10) Year Period: NIOSH 1993		
Occupation	**Number**	**Rate**
Transport	1,500	1.50
Laborers	1,480	1.48
Sales	1,360	1.36
Service	970	0.97
Executive, Administrator, Manager	900	0.90
Agriculture, Fisheries, Forestry	490	0.49
Crafts	420	0.42
Professional, Specialist	260	0.26
Machine Operators	200	0.20
Clerical	180	0.18
Technical, Support	120	0.12

Source: NIOSH (1993, August). *Fatal Injuries to Workers in the United States, 1980-1989: A Decade of Surveillance,* DHHS (NIOSH) No. 93-108, Cincinnati, OH.

The NIOSH study results indicate that persons in such occupations as sales, service, and management experience a high fatality rate due to homicides. The leading cause of death among persons in retail trade, services, finance, insurance, and real estate was homicide.

The high number of OVC homicides for retail and service industry occupations as indicated by NIOSH was supported by additional research conducted by Davis (1987), Hales, Seligman, Newman, and Timbrook (1988), and Kraus (1987) which concluded that retail and service industries experienced the highest number of work-related homicide deaths. They attributed this to greater exposure of these groups to the public and the necessity for the exchange of money, which may increase the risk of occupational homicide.

Part of the NIOSH study focused specifically on females as victims of work-related homicides and suggested that although women traditionally have experienced low rates of work-related injuries resulting in death, they are more likely to die as victims of violence, than from any other type of work-related injury. This is cause for alarm because the leading cause of workplace death for women was homicide. Women were 39 percent more likely than men to be the victims of workplace homicide. Men accounted for 56 percent of the civilian workforce and for 94 percent of all fatal occupational injuries. The rates of occupational homicide by gender demonstrate that the highest rates for both men and women occur in retail trade and personal services. Men employed in public administration are also subject to a high rate of homicide (see Table 1.3). The NIOSH study also showed that occupational fatality rates for homicide increased with age.

Another significant epidemiological study that examined work-related homicides appeared in the *American Journal of Public Health* in 1987. In this study, Kraus (1987) examined the California State Computer Mortality File for work-related homicides. Aware of the inherent problems in the coded portions of the death certificate, Kraus developed an algorithm to search death certificates for three unique factors: "injury at work," "injury at a work location," and "pertinent external-cause-of-death codes."

The algorithm for identifying work-related homicide deaths consisted of four separate steps. The first step required a search of the file for all homicide deaths of California residents from 1979 through 1981. The next step involved identifying the homicides that were work-related. If the death certificate indicated both an "injury at work" and a homicide at an industrial, office, or farm location, then the third step was undertaken. The third step involved examining a written copy of the actual case. The case was reviewed for evidence of a work-related activity. The final step was to read the narrative description of the circumstances of death in the coroner's report.

When the data were analyzed for patterns with regard to gender and age, no age-specific pattern was found in the rates for females. However, the rate of homicide appeared to be slightly higher for males aged 30-64 compared to younger men. The occupational homicide rate for women was one-fourth that of men. The rate of work-related homicide among employed women was five per million compared to 22 per million among men during the years 1979-81 in California.

Table 1.3
Occupational Homicides by Gender

Occupational Homicide: Numbers And Average Annual Industry Specific Work-Related Homicide Rates Per 100,000 Workers Aged 16-64, By Gender: NIOSH 1993			
Type of Industry	**Number of Workers Killed**	**Rate Per 100,000**	
		Female	**Male**
Agriculture, Fisheries, Mining, Forestry	10	.5	1.2
Construction	18	.9	1.1
Manufacturing	40	.9	.1
Transportation, Communication, Public Utility	30	.3	1.9
Wholesale Trade	15	.7	1.6
Retail Trade	141	1.1	5.3
Finance, Insurance, Real Estate	9	.5	3.8
Business/Repair	41	.5	3.8
Personal Services	13	1.5	4.1
Entertainment, Recreation	5	0	1.6
Professional/Related	25	.2	1.1
Public Administration	44	.5	4.5
Total	391	7.6	30.1

Source: NIOSH (1993, August). *Fatal Injuries to Workers in the United States, 1980-1989: A Decade of Surveillance,* DHHS (NIOSH) No. 93-108, Cincinnati, OH.

Industry-specific work-related homicide results were similar to that found in the 1993 NIOSH study. There was a greater number of homicides in the retail trade, business and repair, personal service, and public administration industries. The occupations that were found to have the highest incidence of homicides were service, technical/sales, and managerial/professional. Service occupations for both men and women had the highest rates for work-related homicides. As in a number of other studies, Kraus found that workers who are in occupations or industries that require frequent public contact involving the exchange of money, particularly during evening hours, have the highest risk of homicide.

Unlike the 1993 NIOSH data, Kraus (1987) was able to identify specific "hour-of-injury" in approximately 73 percent of the cases. His findings indicate that about 60 percent of all homicides with known injury times occurred from 3:00 p.m. to 3:00 a.m. with the peak hour being from 11:00 p.m. to midnight. A pattern with regard to the type of weapon also emerged from Kraus' study. Similar to the findings of the NIOSH study and our research, Kraus found firearms to be the most frequently used weapon. In Kraus' study, firearms accounted for 77 percent of all work-related homicides. However, women were more likely to be killed by cutting or stabbing instruments.

In spite of the fact that accurate numbers of work-related homicides are not known in the United States, if the rates found by his study were applied nationwide, Kraus estimated that there could be approximately 1,600 work-related murders occurring annually in this country.

In addition to the studies previously mentioned, numerous non-scientific works have surfaced that have impacted the perception of OVC. One of the more commonly cited sources is Kinney and Johnson's (1993) handbook titled *Breaking Point*, in which he states that murder by employees had "doubled or tripled" since 1989.

The Bureau of Labor Statistics released its first Census of Fatal Occupational Injuries, which concluded that for 1992, homicide was the second leading cause of death in the workplace, after transportation-related accidents. Soon after the census was released, another research report was released by Northwestern National Life Insurance Company (1993), in Minneapolis, Minnesota. This data revealed that approximately 2.2 million workers had been physically attacked on the job in the 12 months ending July 1993. Within the year, the Department of Justice had published its first report on nonfatal workplace violence. The data was taken from ongoing research of crime victim surveys collected from 1987 through 1992. The Justice Department concluded that nearly one million workers annually fall prey to nonfatal violence on the job (Maguire, Pastore & Flanagan, 1993). It is not surprising that workplace violence has been described as a problem of epidemic proportions.

The Society for Human Resource Management completed a study of 479 workplaces over the last five years. The results indicated that there were approximately 160 incidents of violence. Of these cases, more than one-half involved employees as the offender. Karl Seger (1993), of Associated Corporate Consultants, Incorporated, surveyed 32 U.S. companies and found 60 incidents of workplace violence, 44 of which were violent threats, 10 of which were assaults, and six of which were murders.

Two studies conducted in Texas in 1987, concluded that homicide is a significant lethal occupational injury among women. Work-related injuries that resulted in fatalities from 1975-1984 were examined and the data indicated that 53 percent of 348 women were murdered (Davis, Honchar & Suarez, 1987). In contrast, only 13 percent of the fatally injured men were homicide victims (Davis, 1987). Another commonly cited insurance study (Northwestern, 1993), was intended to be broad in scope in order to determine what factors made workers feel unsafe in their work environments. Their study found that one in four workers was harassed, threatened, or physically attacked. However, the survey response rate was 29 percent, which is considered low, and was based on interviews with only 15 people, thus posing threats to reliability and validity. Northwestern, however, used the results to estimate that 2.2 million people had been physically attacked at work in the 12 months preceding the survey. Daun Castilo, an epidemiologist with NIOSH, cautioned that these results "need to be interpreted with caution" (Bell et al., 1990:3048).

As these studies are released, they are being criticized and have come under attack for misinterpretation of workplace violence. According to Erik Larson (1994), the Bureau of Labor Statistics ranks homicide as the second leading cause of workplace death. Upon closer scrutiny, however, the statistical study reveals that workplace murder is a rare event. For example, of approximately 121 million people in the workforce in 1993, only 1,063—or one out of 114,000—were killed while at work or on duty. The data varied considerably depending upon occupation. Persons facing the greatest risk appeared to be those in management. The risk however appears slight with the chances being one in 226,000 (Larson, 1994). However, NIOSH estimated the risk for management as 0.90 per 100,000 for a 10-year period while their report of overall homicide deaths per year was slightly less than that reported by the Bureau of Labor Statistics. The NIOSH study also showed homicide as a relatively rare event, representing only 12 percent of occupational injury deaths for a 10-year period.

Some of the conflict between the results of these studies can be attributed to an overly broad definition given to workplace violence. For example, the Department of Justice's 1994 study, which found that one million workers are victims of nonfatal workplace violence each year, failed to determine if the offender was an employee or ex-employee, whether the crime occurred at work or while on duty, and whether the victims knew their attackers. The Department of Justice's study did not find any evidence that workplace violence was on the rise. Interestingly, it did find that 33 percent of the crimes, which ranged from threats of assault to rape, occurred most often in parking lots, garages, or on public property. Only 14 percent occurred in an office, plant, or warehouse. This data also includes attacks on police officers, prison guards, and convenience-store clerks (Maguire & Pastore, 1995).

According to the New York State Public Employees Federation, a union representing 56,000 white-collar professionals working for state corrections and health facilities, incidents of violence or homicide have been overestimated (*New York Times,* 1993). Beginning in 1989, the Federation provided its members with Assault, Trauma, and Captivity Insurance. Using claims against this policy as a measurement of workplace violent incidents, Richard Doucette, administrator of the program, indicated that he had dealt with only one or two claims per year involving violence by a co-worker or ex-worker.

Unfortunately, as is the case with much research, the findings often become separated from their "statistical moorings." The danger of this type of analysis is that all too often it is self-serving. Those individuals who stand to gain the most from the research results are the very "experts" that further their own professional consulting careers. This should not, however, diminish the importance of the issue of violence in the workplace which is founded in more seemingly reliable research, such as that conducted by NIOSH.

There has also been criticism of the media's reporting of postal incidents. The implication is that the postal service has a higher incidence of workplace violence than most other organizations. The statistics indicate that murder was the second-highest cause of death on the job for postal workers and the third highest cause of death for all workers. A firearm was the most common slaying weapon and postal employees were more likely to be killed by a co-worker than by nonemployees of the postal service. Between 1983-1987, 57 percent of work-related slayings in the postal service were committed by co-workers or former colleagues (Kadaba, 1993:F1).

Consequently, postal authorities are taking measures to respond to these highly publicized incidents. Currently they are conducting an extensive psychological study to develop a psychological profile of employees prone to violence.

Dan Mihalko, spokesman for the Postal Inspection Service, the law enforcement arm of the postal service, says that the study will examine about 350 cases of postal workers' assaults including verbal threats as well as physical attacks, which occurred from 1989 to 1992. According to Mihalko, the 350 cases represent a sampling of about 2,000 incidents meeting these criteria, which were located in the service's files. Mihalko states that although postal officials are not sure how they will use the findings of the study, emphasis will be placed upon pre-employment screening. Postal employees express concerns that the study may affect broad groups of employees and job applicants, particularly military veterans.

Criticisms of Previous Workplace Violence Research

Criticism has been levied at the scientific data presented in previous research. For example, the NIOSH research has been criticized as incomplete because it relies solely on recorded death certificates, which do not provide statistics on the various types and results of OVC. For example, data on physical injuries are not collected nationally, nor are data that represent emotional trauma associated with injuries or rapes. NIOSH acknowledges that the research results are limited because of the use of death certificates, due to frequent inaccuracies in information included on the death certificate, and the fact that states are sometimes unable to identify and retrieve death certificates that should be included in the research. NIOSH reports that homicides and suicides were under-reported in their project data. Under-reporting of work-related fatalities, due to the incorrect identification as to whether or not the injury occurred at work, is estimated to be between 12 percent and 33 percent, as indicated in a summarization of numerous state data (Bell et al., 1990).

Moreover, it is estimated that employment data is missing for approximately 20 percent of occupational information, such as job description or position, and 13 percent of industry data, such as the type of facility (Bell et al., 1990). A workshop sponsored by NIOSH and the Center for Disease Control in Washington, D.C., in July 1990, identified nine common inherent limitations in the available OVC data sources (Jenkins, Lagne & Kisher, 1992). Only one of these limitations, if corrected, would significantly improve the research from the perspective of providing a basis for understanding the nature and causes of workplace violence. Death certificates do not lend themselves to providing the type of epidemiological information necessary to describe the circumstances surrounding an OVC. Therefore, there often is not enough detail to determine the sequence of events that ultimately end in an OVC. Without information on the incident, offenders, and victims it is difficult to gain much indication of the nature and causes of workplace violence.

The difficulty with the majority of the previous studies of workplace violence is the fact that the data sources that were used tend to be unreliable and/or fail to include needed information for understanding the incidents, offenders, and victims of workplace violence. These criticisms are valid for both the most detailed studies available, NIOSH and the California study, due to their dependence on information available from death certificates. Therefore, other sources of information should be identified and examined to analyze the phenomenon of OVC.

One source that may prove useful for this purpose is the new National Incident Based Reporting System (NIBRS). NIBRS, unlike the Uniform Crime Report (UCR), provides a more detailed reporting system for criminal incidents. Most policing agencies use the UCR to summarize the number of specific offenses and submit aggregate counts of arrest data in monthly summary reports either directly to the Federal Bureau of Investigation or indirectly through state programs. This system does not require that the offense arrest data is linked to previously submitted incident reports. In addition to the numbers of arrests, data include the clearances, types and values of stolen and recovered property, and the age, sex, race, and ethnic origin of people who are arrested. The National Incident Based Reporting System differs from the UCR in that the NIBRS system uses "incident-based" reporting rather than a summary. It provides a more detailed reporting system and also includes a section on location of incident, reporting the type of facility where each offense took place. Such information would allow researchers to determine whether or not the incident occurred in the workplace.

NIBRS requires law enforcement agencies to collect detailed data regarding individual crime incidents and arrests and submit them in separate "reports" using prescribed data elements and data values to describe each incident and arrest. The significance of this to workplace violence is that for the first time a law enforcement reporting system will collect data on the type of location in which a homicide was committed. There is also a section on victims and a category for the relationship(s) of the victim(s) to the offender(s). Overall, there are 52 data elements used in the National Incident Based Reporting System to describe the victims, offenders, arrestees, and circumstances of crimes.

Another important distinction is that the NIBRS does not use the "Hierarchy Rule." This rule is used when more than one crime was committed by the same person or group of persons and the time and space intervals separating the crimes were insignificant. The crime highest in the Crime Index hierarchy is the only one that is reported. The result is that in multiple-crime incidents, (which often applies to workplace violence) the less serious offenses are not reported. NIBRS reports all offenses occurring in an incident. For example, if a disgruntled employee enters the workplace and murders his supervisor, wounds several co-workers and then rapes a female co-worker, under the UCR system, the lesser offense of rape would not be reported. However, with the NIBRS, both homicide and forcible rape would be reported.

NIBRS also provides more detailed information on the victim-offender relationship. The UCR summary reporting system reports this type of data on homicides only. Whereas with NIBRS, the victim's relationship to the offender is reported when the victim was the object of a "Crime Against Person," which would include crimes such as assaults, homicides, kidnaping, abductions, and forcible and unforced sex offenses.

In summary, data that has been used to assess the magnitude of OVC in the workplace comes from a variety of sources, such as NIOSH, the California study, and numerous anecdotal works, none of which provide the kind of data which is necessary for understanding workplace violence incidents. Although the Uniform Crime Reports could be a valuable source of information, its utility is limited by the fact that there is no way to determine whether a workplace connection exists and reporting by agencies is voluntary. The National Incident Based Reporting System, on the other hand, has the potential of contributing significantly to the existing body of research and is worth future examination. However, it will be several years before the NIBRS database will have historical data for examining the phenomenon of workplace violence.

Due to the lack of readily available mechanisms to study the incidents, offenders, and victims of workplace violence, the authors of this text chose another direction to systematically examine and provide more insight to the nature and causes of workplace violence.

The Current Research

In hopes of providing a more complete picture of the phenomenon of workplace violence, the research presented in this text uses press releases from the wire services of Associated Press (AP) and United Press International (UPI) as its data source. In an earlier study, Southerland and Collins (1994) examined news reports of workplace violence incidents in the five major U.S. newspapers by utilizing the Newspaper Index. As a result of that study, they determined that newspaper accounts provided much more information regarding workplace violence incidents than was available in research documented earlier in this chapter. They also found that the local newspaper had more detailed reports of the incident, offender, and victims than was found in other newspapers. The present study is an extension of their previous work. Initially the authors planned to search for local newspaper accounts of workplace violence incidents. However, without an initial list of all incidents by location, there was no apparent way to accomplish this task without also obtaining all the reports of each incident as it was reported throughout the country. Therefore, we chose to use AP and UPI to establish a list of workplace violence incidents and collect our data from the various wire service reports on each incident.

It can be argued that wire service accounts represent some unknown sample of the population of events being studied; however, due to the nature of these two wire services and the subject under study, we believe the data presented here is as representative as any other method currently available for examining potentially lethal and lethal violence in the workplace setting. More importantly, it provides much more detailed information on the nature and causes of these incidents, their offenders, and victims than previously has been available. AP and UPI are the primary means for news distribution to media sources in the United States. Most news media (print and broadcast) subscribe to one of these two sources or both and provide news coverage to their chosen distributor. Robinson and Sheehan (1983) reported that AP had more than 1,400 newspaper members while UPI had approximately 1,000 clients. They indicate that 95 percent of the 1,700 American dailies subscribe to either AP, UPI, or both and "for the most part, national news in local papers is still wirecopy, cut and pasted to fit between the grocery ads and classifieds" (1983:15). Three studies reached a similar conclusion that 60 to 75 percent of the copy that is printed in the local press comes from the wires (MacDougall, 1968; Ebring, 1980; Shaw, 1969). Most U.S. cities are small and have only one wire service available due to the fact that there is generally a single newspaper. Therefore, the coverage of AP and UPI should be expected to have some overlap, but fairly significant divergence. Indeed, this is what we found when we compared the workplace violence cases of the two news sources. There were only slightly more than 30 cases that were reported in both sources. Using data from either AP or UPI without the other might seriously have skewed or misrepresented the nature of workplace violence.

AP is a cooperative of member newspapers while UPI is a private company. These two dominating U.S. wire services compete fiercely in domestic as well as international news. Within each agency the decisions on which news stories will be included and which will not are made on a story-by-story basis (Fenby, 1986). Rivers (1964) discussed the fact that mass media critics had been complaining for decades that information was ignored and entertainment emphasized. Some of the leading journalists of that time had also begun to echo the criticism. The driving force for these concerns was, as it still is, the fact of space and time limitations and how those precious resources are allocated to different news items, advertising, and entertainment—the economic realities of publishing and broadcasting. There is nothing new about the phenomenon of selective inclusion in the newspaper nor the wire service world. In his 1927 text, Harwood reported on the decision process for determining what is news by editors of newspapers and by the AP wire service. Even in that time when life was by all accounts much less fast-paced and simpler, he wrote: "Every editor admits that far more things happen in a day than any paper can possibly print; and those journals which try to cover fully the great range of the day's happenings are very likely to bewilder their readers with the quantity of their wares" (1927:39). The type of violent behavior we chose to examine for this text is very likely to be included by the wire service as a part of its service to local newspapers while an individual newspaper may choose not to commit its space to print the report. Therefore, we believe the wire service to be the most representative primary source for data regarding workplace violence that is currently available for a study of the phenomenon over time.

Much of the information reported in the AP and UPI news releases was based on police accounts of the incidents. Thus, these incidents were a matter of public record and public interest. There are most certainly cases that were missed due to one of the following reasons: they were submitted to neither AP nor UPI, they were missed in the Key Words in Context Search, or the incident was settled so successfully within the workplace setting that official sources were not notified. The data presented here most surely underestimates the frequency with which potentially lethal incidents occur but are resolved without incident.

While there are limitations with the present data as with any research, it provides information on offenders, the location of the incident, and various organizational variables which are not available in any other source of information to date.

The current research uses content analysis as the means to examine cases of potentially lethal and lethal workplace violence. Researchers have developed various definitions of content analysis. For example, Marshall and Rossman (1989) indicate that content analysis is used for making objective inferences while systematically identifying specified characteristics (Marshall & Rossman, 1989). Weber (1990) described content analysis as a data reduction technique with which researchers can make enormous amounts of information more manageable and at the same time useful, providing for practical application. Berelson's (1952) definition is perhaps the most widely accepted, defining content analysis as a "research technique for the objective, systematic, and quantitative description of the manifest content of communication" (Berelson, 1952:489). In other words, content analysis is a method for reducing large amounts of data into a useful format for understanding a given problem. This data then, can be used to develop practical solutions.

Although content analysis has been used in a variety of disciplines, it was first used in journalism to study communication. Numerous researchers studying forms of sociology, literature, public opinion, propaganda, adult education, psychology, and even military intelligence have benefitted from the use of this technique (Berelson, 1952).

Data for content analysis may come from various media such as textbooks, novels, newspapers, and other official documents. As stated previously, the data for this research include articles taken from Associated Press (AP) and United Press International (UPI) databases. Since neither AP nor UPI databases are indexed, we used a "Key Words in Context" search to determine the articles for which we would obtain a full copy. Most frequently identified key words include: kill, murder, rampage, violence, homicide, shoot, fatal, shot, injury, co-worker, worker, employee, and supervisor. All articles were obtained regarding each incident. Therefore, the available information spanned the full potential of such cases, for instance, articles included those from the beginning reports of the incident to the conclusion of the trial process and the execution of the convicted individual in some incidents. Once the full copy of all articles were received, they were screened and sorted by case name. Initially, the researchers screened articles to include every article in which the incident appeared to have the potential for lethal violence, the incident was work-related in some way, it involved at least one offender with some relationship to the workplace, or the incident occurred in a workplace but was committed in conjunction with another crime. After all articles had been sorted into incident files, the researchers were able to distinguish six categories of violent incidents.

Category I—*Definite cases of potentially lethal workplace violence.* These cases met each of the following three conditions:

1. Lethal violence was possibly based on an examination of the scenario. It was not necessary to have an injury to meet this condition.

2. There must be some connection between an assailant and the workplace. The connection might be an "intimate other" who was employed there or that the assailant was a customer.

3. At least some potentially violent action must take place in the "workplace."

Category II—*Work-related cases*. These were the same as Category I except *all* violent action took place outside the workplace.

Category III—*Suspected cases*. These cases were not confirmed as having a workplace connection but police or others indicated that the possibility of a work connection was being examined.

Category IV—*Possible cases*. It was suspected by the researchers that these were workplace-related cases, but there was too little information in the article(s) to put the incident in another category.

Category V—*"Terrorist Acts" in the workplace*. The site of the violence was random. There was no connection between any assailant and the workplace. An example of such cases is a robbery or other type of incident in which an offender randomly selects the workplace to use for lethal violence.

Category VI—*The "Organization Itself" as murderer*. The organization knowingly placed employees in danger without the employee being aware of the potentially lethal situation.

For purposes of this research, the cases were screened and the data reported here includes only Category I incidents.

The development of a comprehensive coding scheme is vital for accurate content analysis. The coding scheme is usually produced based on a review of the literature and an examination of a random sample of the data. This method was followed for developing the data collection instruments used in this study (see Appendices 1, 2, and 3). The coding scheme consists of variables that provide a description of the subject matter and/or answers to research questions. Variables for this research include characteristics of the incidents, offenders, and victims as descriptors of potentially lethal workplace violence.

Context of the Current Research

Research examining workplace violence is limited. Previous data sources include death certificates from each states' vital statistics reporting unit, workers compensation claims, OSHA fatality files, and organization surveys. To date, there has been no other research using newspaper articles as a data source. This medium was chosen in hopes of portraying a more detailed picture of workplace violence, specifically potentially lethal workplace violence.

Previous works examined primarily incidents of fatalities in the workplace. This research examines not only fatalities, but also minor and serious injuries as well as threats. Additionally, previous works have examined incidents that include those that may have been committed by persons who are not employees and occurred in conjunction with a crime, such as robbery. This research excludes those incidents that involve the commission of a crime that is not work-related. In the data collected for this text the authors found 246 cases of workplace violence occurring over a 13-year period, which were perpetrated by someone with a relationship to the workplace. We have focused our attention on violence that has been committed by someone with a known link to the workplace where the violence occurred because such incidents had the greatest potential for preventive action.

2 A Typology of Workplace Violence Incidents

This chapter presents the results of our research and current understanding of the nature and causes of workplace violence as we have defined it. The chapter begins with a typology of workplace violence, then a discussion of criminological theory that is relevant to workplace violence, and a presentation of demographic variation in violence. The final sections of the chapter are devoted to a presentation of profiles of incidents, offenders, and victims of workplace violence.

The Typology

The data developed from the content analysis of workplace violence incidents, as described in Chapter 1, revealed a clear typology. There are two dimensions for classifying these cases. One dimension is the *site*—the type of workplace in which the incident occurs; the second is the *offender/workplace relationship*—the relationship of the offender to the workplace setting. Each dimension has three levels.

The *site* dimension can be classified into three categories: nongovernment service organizations, government and other institutions, and manufacturing industries. The labels used for the categories of the site dimension are: "service," "government/institution," and "manufacturing." The vast majority of cases (89%) fell into one of these three categories. The site dimension is an ordinal variable based on the level of public contact required of employees. Service organizations are designed to be direct service providers to the public. The government/institution category of organizations also provide public service but have somewhat less direct contact than those organizations classified as service providers. Manufacturing organizations have little direct contact with the public.

The *offender/workplace relationship* dimension can be classified into three categories of offenders: the employee (including all levels of employment for the organization as well as those who were former employees), the customer, and the domestic-related offender. The labels used for the offender/workplace relationship dimension are: "employee," "customer," and "domestic-related." The domestic-related offenders had some form of intimate relationship to an organizational employee. They might have been a spouse, lover, or relative of an employee. Most cases (82%) fell into one of these three categories. The offender/workplace relationship dimension is also an ordinal variable based on the offender's relationship to the workplace. This dimension reflects the relative degree of connection between the offender and the workplace. Employees had the greatest connection to the workplace because nearly all of them were, at one time, full-time workers; customers were less connected; and the domestic-related offenders typically had only an indirect connection to the workplace.

Table 2.1 shows the typology with the percent of cases, for which information was available on both dimensions, in each cell. *Employees in service organizations* is the single largest type of incident. This type is twice that of the next two most frequent types, *employees in government/institutions* and *employees in manufacturing,* both of which were almost equally represented with 18 and 16 percent, respectively. Customers comprise 16 percent of the cases with somewhat more being *customers of service* than being *customers of government/institutions.* There are no customer offenders for the manufacturing category. This finding is not surprising since there is very little direct contact with customers for manufacturing organizations. Domestic-related offenders make up 9 percent of the total cases and are distributed mostly in the service category.

Table 2.1
Typology of Workplace Violence

Offender/Work Relationship	Site of Incident			
	Government/ Service	Institution	Manufacturing	Total
Employee	41%	18%	16%	75%
Customer	10%	6%	—	16%
Domestic Related	6%	2%	1%	9%
Total	57%	26%	17%	100%

Source: Compiled by M. Southerland, P. Collins & K. Scarborough.

Criminological Explanations

The three primary causes that have been used to explain violent crime are biological, psychological, and sociological causes. Monahan (1994), in his synopsis of the causes of violence, concluded that violence does not have one root cause but many tangled roots. The National Academy of Sciences has found no proven biological risk factors for future violence. Sociological factors such as region of the country, size of the community, age, gender, race, and poverty are related to the incidence of violence. There is much interrelation between these variables, making it difficult to know which factors are important and which are irrelevant. For example, if poverty is taken into account when examining violence, the effect of race decreases significantly (Monahan, 1994). Monahan discounts the importance of mental disorder as a factor in violence since the evidence indicates that serious mental disorders account for an insignificant amount of American violence, at most, 3 percent. However, he indicates that the family has the most potential effect on controlling violence through its influence on the psychological development of the child.

Control of "impulsive" temperament and aggressive behavior of children is best begun with the family, according to Monahan (1994). Monahan further indicates that both biological and sociological factors influence the nature of the family, yet the family might best redirect some of these influences. Nevertheless, little of what he offers in terms of family influences to reduce the violent nature of individuals has consequence for the perpetrators of workplace violence. Our study found that most of the offenders were "normal" individuals, not prone to violent acts. Therefore, these offenders were not typical perpetrators of violence. Some other explanation(s) must be found.

The theories of crime causation that appear most relevant for explaining workplace violence are routine activities theory, general theory of self-control, containment theory, strain theory, and those theories that explain parricide (the killing of a parent or other family member by a child) and domestic violence. These theories may be applicable for examining workplace violence for the following reasons:

1. *General Theory of Self-Control*—Many of the offenders appeared to have reached their frustration threshhold and their typical self-control was no longer sufficient to keep them from committing an act of violence.

2. *Routine Activities Theory*—Routine activities theory is relevant to the workplace victims in that the whereabouts of the victims were known by the offenders and the victims were going about their normal duties when the acts of violence occurred. This might also explain why the incidents of domestic violence occurred in the workplace. The offender knew where their intended victim could be found and sought them out at the workplace.

3. *Containment Theory*—For those employees who use their position to gain the necessary information from which to commit robbery, the motivation appears to be greed. The lethal violence in such types of cases may result from a desire of the offender to protect himself or herself from detection or to keep from being apprehended at the scene (Felson & Messner, 1996).

4. *Strain Theory*—Most of the employees and all of the customers who commit workplace violence believe they have been mistreated by the organization and/or specific members within it.

5. *Parricide Theory*—Employee violence against those in the workplace has several similar characteristics to those found in studies of parricide.

6. *Domestic Violence Theory*—Domestic-related offenders most often express a loss of control over the individual who has rejected their "love" or who appears to have "rebelled" against their authority. Committing the act of violence in the victim's workplace gives the offender a substantial degree of control over the fate of their intended victim.

A brief review of each theory follows.

General Theory or *Self-Control Theory.* Gottfredson and Hirschi (1990) claim that their "general theory," or self-control theory, explains the tendency to commit all crimes. Their theory assumes that offenders have little control over their own behavior and desires. When the need for immediate gratification outweighs long-term interests, crime occurs. Crime is a function of poor self-control. Inadequate socialization and poor child-rearing practices, coupled with poor attachment, increase the probability of impulsive and uncontrolled acts. For workplace violence incidents, the offenders were not "criminals," but their self-control was overridden by the "pressure" to resolve the "problem" as they saw it. The offender's long-term interests reached a low enough priority to allow his/her "immediate gratification" to take over.

Routine Activities Theory. Cohen and Felson (1979 and 1993) use the routine activities theory to explain direct-contact predatory violations in which someone intentionally takes or damages the person or property of another. They argue that there are three minimal elements of direct-contact predatory violations: (1) motivated offenders, (2) suitable targets, and (3) the absence of capable guardians against a violation. The lack of any one of these elements is sufficient to prevent an occurrence of such crime. They also argue that "guardianship by ordinary citizens . . . as they go about their routine activities" (Cohen & Felson, 1993:270) may be one of the most neglected and important keys to control of direct-contact predatory crime. Predatory crime may be understood as "a byproduct of freedom and prosperity as they manifest themselves in the routine activities of everyday life" (1993:274). Cohen and Felson (1993) also believe that when circumstances are favorable for carrying out the criminal act, such knowledge may contribute to the criminal inclination in the long run by rewarding those inclinations. "Substantial increases in the opportunity to carry out predatory violations may have undermined society's mechanisms for social control" (1993:274).

Workplace violence fits the definition of a direct-contact predatory crime. It also fits the three minimal elements: (1) there are motivated offenders; (2) there are targets in the workplace who are the perceived "enemy(ies)" of the offender, and (3) the offender believes no one will be able to stop him/her from committing the act. Indeed, almost all offenders either kill themselves or turn themselves in to the police after committing the act. They are not concerned with "getting away with" the crime but in successfully executing it.

Containment Theory. Reckless distinguished between two forms of containment that provide defense, protection, or insulation against delinquency or criminality. *Outer containment* is the structural buffer that holds a person within the social bounds and consists of a variety of factors including a set of reasonable limitations and responsibilities, a social role that guides the person's activities, an opportunity for the individual to achieve status; a sense of belonging and identification with the members of the group, and provisions for alternative ways and means of satisfaction when one or more of the typical means is closed. *Inner containment* is personal control that is ensured by such factors as a good self-concept, self-control, a strong ego, a well-developed conscience, a high frustration tolerance, and a high sense of responsibility. Reckless suggests that criminality results when the offender's internal pushes toward crime (such as hostility) and external pressures toward crime (such as unemployment or blocked opportunities), fail to be controlled by his/her inner and outer containment (Adler, Mueller & Laufer, 1995). Workplace violence incidents often seem to reflect a breakdown in the outer containment along with internal pushes of hostility or anger and external pressures of job loss, blocked opportunity for promotion, or being wronged by the organization or its employees. The external pressures in these cases are contributing factors to the internal pushes. The combination of these overwhelms the inner containment of the individual and allows the violent incident to be considered and then carried out.

Strain Theory. This theory assumes that people are law-abiding, but when under great pressure they will resort to crime. The source of this pressure is a disparity between the individual's goals and means to achieve those goals. The disparity between goals and the means to achieve them results in frustration, leading to strain. For this theory the social structure is the root of the crime problem (Adler, Mueller & Laufer, 1995); this is not consistent with our findings on workplace violence. Therefore, strain theory in its "true" form is not applicable. However, if it is applied to the frustration of goals and means for individual workers, it does apply when the various frustrations of all three categories of offenders are examined. Many of the offenders in each category (employee, customer, and domestic-related) were responding to a frustration or "strain" of goals and means to achieve them. It appears that for most of them, in their own minds at least, there was no recourse but to commit this act of violence.

Parricide Theory. Twelve characteristics associated with adolescents who kill family members, particularly their fathers, were identified by Heide (1995) based on a review of eight classic clinical studies, the empirical comparison of these studies by Corder, Ball, Haizlip, Rollins, and Beaumont (1976) and her own research. These 12 characteristics follow:

1. There was a pattern of family violence, some of which was physical but other was psychological;

2. The adolescents attempts to get help failed;

3. The adolescents failed to escape the family situation;

4. Parricide offenders were isolated from others and had fewer outlets than other youths;

5. The family situation became increasingly intolerable prior to the homicidal event;

6. The adolescents felt increasingly helpless to deal with the home situation;

7. The inability of the adolescents to cope with the familial situation led to a loss of control;

8. Parricide offenders were criminally unsophisticated, having no prior criminal history;

9. The easy availability of a gun was a critical factor in the occurrence of the homicide;

10. There was alcoholism or heavy drinking in the homes in which parents were slain by an adolescent;

11. The adolescent parricide offender may have been in a dissociative state during or after the homicide; and

12. The victim's death was perceived as a relief by the offender and other surviving family members and in many cases there was an apparent absence of remorse.

If not physically abused, many workplace violence offenders perceived themselves as having been emotionally and/or psychologically mistreated. That mistreatment was of a long-term nature. There was evidence that these offenders believed they had done everything they could do to resolve the problem and had no options available but to resort to violence. They were relieved that the "deed" had been accomplished. There was little indication that such offenders were in a dissociative state; however, they appeared focused on the task they had been "driven" to accomplish. Weapon availability was an important factor since most of these incidents were committed with firearms. The workplace offenders, for the most part, had no prior criminal record. There is little evidence to indicate that the workplace violence offender is a "loner;" however, these offenders appear to have few close friends in whom they confided within the workplace. The helplessness in dealing with their situations may be one of the most crucial likenesses to the parricide offender.

Domestic Violence. One study of spousal homicides suggests that they are the result of a husband's efforts to control his wife and the wife's efforts to retain her independence (Daly & Wilson, 1988). Livingston (1996) presents two themes in wife abuse. One is jealousy in which the abusive man may turn to deadly violence over perceived or real infidelity on the part of his wife. Male dominance is the other theme. Here the real issue is power, the man's goal is the establishment of his own dominance and the humiliation and degradation of the woman. Any of several factors can contribute to his heightened anxiety over his position of dominance and trigger the violent episode—alcohol or drugs, lack of money, social isolation, or stress from setbacks resulting from unemployment or illness. The power issue in violence is not only evident in domestic violence but for other types. Violence, at least for the serial murderer interviewed by Hickey (1991), was a means of reasserting his superiority in retaliation for real or perceived slights by the victim. "Violence...had been reinforced as a means of taking control, as a means of getting even, getting even with the world" (1991:208). Violence was "...a means of coping with stress" (1991:209). Violence was an adaptive strategy, rationally conceived to satisfy his needs and/or desires. The dominance issue also may be at work in motivating the workplace violence incidence in which someone else gets the promotion; this may be particularly true when it is a female rather than a male who is promoted.

Demographic Variation in Violence

Violence is subject to regional variation. Nelsen, Corzine, and Huff-Corzine (1994) examined regional homicide rates in the United States for the years 1979-1981 and found the overall homicide rate was highest in the South, while the white homicide rate was highest in the West, and the homicide rate for blacks was highest in the West and lowest in the South. When they examined the data, controlling for population density (central city, suburban, and nonmetropolitan areas), their findings changed. They found no distinct regional pattern of homicide rates for blacks, yet whites in the South were the most likely victims of homicide.

Nisbett (1993) found that the murder rate in the South is almost twice that of the Northeast while the robbery rate for the Northeast is almost twice that of the South. Street violence is committed disproportionately by the poor and unemployed (Monahan, 1994). This is directly contradicted in our data regarding violence in the workplace where the offenders are predominately individuals employed in the workplace. The overwhelming majority (90%) of those arrested for violent crime are men (Monahan, 1994) a finding that was supported in our data where men committed 86 percent of the incidents. The smaller the community, the lower the rate of violence (Reiss & Roth, 1993). We had no means for assessing the size of the workplace. The arrest and victimization rate for violent crime for blacks is about six times higher than for whites (Reiss & Roth, 1993). Race was almost never reflected in the accounts available to us. Official violent crime rates underestimate the actual rate of violence in America, particularly that violence which occurs within the family (Monahan, 1993).

Supplemental data on murder victims provided by contributing law enforcement agencies for 22,076 or the estimated 23,305 murders in 1994 showed that 79 percent of murder victims were males, 88 percent were at least 18 years old, 47 percent were 20 to 34 years old, and 51 percent were black while 47 percent were white (U.S. Department of Justice, 1995). The rate of victimization for individuals aged 18 to 24 was more than twice that of any other category (23.6 per 100,000). Considering the rates of murder and nonnegligent manslaughter victimization in the United States for 1992, men were victimized at a rate almost five times that of women (14.2 compared to 3.8) and blacks were victimized at a rate seven times that of whites (35.2 compared to 5.0) (Maguire, Pastore & Flanagan, 1993).

Supplemental data reported for 25,052 murder offenders in 1994 showed that 91 percent were male, 84 percent were over 18 years old, 69 percent were ages 17-34, 56 percent were black, and 42 percent white.

Murder is most often intraracial, with 94 percent of black victims slain by black offenders and 84 percent of white victims slain by white offenders. However, murder is typically not intragender. Males were most often killed by males (88%) while 90 percent of all female victims were killed by males (U.S. Department of Justice, 1995).

Roth (1994) reviewed the findings of the National Academy of Sciences Panel on the Understanding and Control of Violent Behavior and found that murder rates had been as high as they are now earlier in this century—around 1931-34 and again in 1979-81. The difference in murder victimization rates for blacks compared to whites appears primarily to reflect conditions in low-income neighborhoods and tends to disappear in high-income neighborhoods (Roth, 1994). In nearly 40 percent of all murders, the relationship between the victims and their killers is unknown to the police at the time the statistics are reported (Roth, 1994). Strangers account for 20 percent of the offenders, intimate partners or family members for 30 percent, and other acquaintances for the remaining 50 percent. Women face only about one-third the murder risk faced by men. However, women are four times more likely to be killed by intimates or spouses than men (Roth, 1994).

Roth (1994) used Reiss and Roth's (1993) matrix for organizing risk factors for violent behavior to examine two specific murder cases. The diversity of these two cases illustrated the importance of viewing a violent event as the outcome of a long chain of preceding events. To prevent the violent act, intervention might have successfully occurred at any one of several links. The tendency of researchers and others examining incidents of homicidal violence is often to look at the murder incident as the product of a set of factors that can be ranked in order of importance. Roth (1994) indicated that ranking of factors is not illuminating for identifying a broad set of intervention points at which violent deaths might be prevented before they occur. Instead he recommends looking at the full incident to identify all potential intervention points. The potential intervention points cannot be identified without a complete description of the incident, as well as, the events leading up to the lethal violence. Our work is important because it is a first step in quantitatively and qualitatively examining full incidents of potentially lethal violence in the workplace setting.

Profile of Workplace Violence Incidents

The 246 incidents or cases of workplace violence can be characterized as follows. Incidents were more likely to occur in the South, on a Wednesday in October 1988 at 9:00 a.m., 12:00 p.m., or 3:00 p.m. Incidents occurred most frequently in office buildings, followed very closely by restaurants. These incidents rarely involved alcohol or drug use, rarely were committed in conjunction with another crime, and rarely were committed during or immediately following a job action. The incidents, on an extremely limited number of occasions involved a love triangle or murder-for-hire. A firearm was the weapon most commonly used.

Region of Occurrence. The South had the highest number of workplace violence incidents, followed closely by the West (see Figure 2.1). These findings are similar to those reported by Nelsen, et al. (1994), for general homicide. No significant differences were found when the *region* in which incidents occurred was compared by the type of site, the total number of injuries, and the total number of people killed. These findings suggest that we can be confident in the applicability of the findings to a variety of sites by type and geography.

Figure 2.1
Region of Occurrence

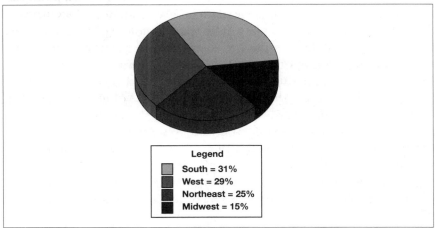

Source: Compiled by M. Southerland, P. Collins & K. Scarborough.

Timing. Incidents most frequently occurred in October and least frequently in August (see Figure 2.2). In terms of seasonality, the highest percentages of cases occurred in the Winter months, December-February (30%) and the Fall months, September-November (29%). The lowest percentage occurred during Summer.

Figure 2.2
Incidents by Month

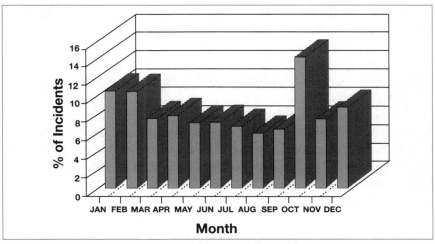

Source: Compiled by M. Southerland, P. Collins & K. Scarborough.

Although the electronic databases, from which the articles were drawn, were begun in 1983, and 1983 is used as the starting point for this research, the actual range of years in which the cases occurred is 1976 to 1994. This nearly 20-year time span is the longest examination of workplace violence incidents conducted to date, consequently providing the most comprehensive look at workplace violence. Those incidents that were identified for inclusion in the database, but which occurred before 1983, were often reporting on the trials or the sentencing of offenders. When examining Figure 2.3 for incidents by year, 1983 should be considered the starting point for examining the trends in workplace violence incidents.

Figure 2.3
Incidents by Year

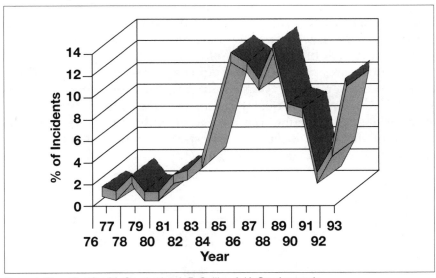

Source: Compiled by M. Southerland, P. Collins & K. Scarborough.

Incidents were broadly distributed by day of the month. The largest numbers of incidents by day were on the 24th day of the month (n=13), followed closely by the 14th (n=12), 6th, 9th and 25th (n=11). Unlike heightened criminal activity, which occurs in relation to pay days (generally the 15th and 30th or last day of the month), these dates do not reflect such a pattern. In fact, the smallest numbers of incidents fell on the 15th and 29th.

An examination of incidents by day of the week showed that 20 percent of the incidents occurred on Wednesday followed by Monday with 18 percent. Although Friday and Saturday are frequently known as high periods for criminal activity, this was not the case here. Violence that occurs in the workplace then, is more likely to occur in the course of the normal Monday through Friday work week. Most incidents occurred during normal working hours, between 9:00 a.m. and 5:00 p.m.

Site. More than one-half of the incidents occurred in service types of workplaces. Government/institution was the next most frequent site accounting for 22 percent of the cases. Third was manufacturing/warehouse sites making up 14 percent of the cases. Considering specific sites, the most frequent location for workplace violence incidents was an office building (13% of incidents; 12% of victims) and the next most frequent was restaurants (11% of incidents; 16% of victims) and government agencies (11% of incidents; 10% of victims). The postal service accounted for 4 percent of all incidents and 6 percent of all victims of workplace violence.

Multiple sites are rare in workplace violence. Only 24 of the cases involved multiple sites, indicating that the workplace was merely one stop in a series of incidents, which often involve a private residence belonging to a relative or "intimate" of the offender, as one of the other locations. Almost all workplace violence incidents begin *and* end in the workplace.

Figure 2.4
Incidents by Site

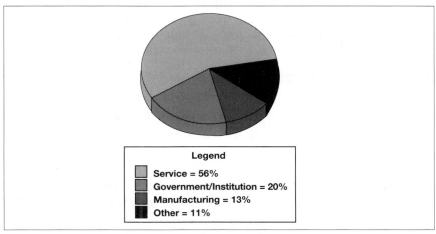

Legend
Service = 56%
Government/Institution = 20%
Manufacturing = 13%
Other = 11%

Source: Compiled by M. Southerland, P. Collins & K. Scarborough.

Number of Offenders. The vast majority (82%) of offenders committed their act of workplace violence alone. The most offenders that ever worked together was five, which occurred only once. Seven percent of the offenders worked in pairs, four percent of the offenders worked in groups of three, while five percent worked in groups of four. There was a total of 282 offenders for all incidents (n=246). Specific offender characteristics are presented in the next section.

Weapon. Several types of weapons were used by offenders in these workplace violence incidents, for example, firearms, hands, explosives, and drugs. In 13 percent of the incidents multiple weapons were used by the assailant(s). The most frequently used weapon was a revolver, accounting for 40 percent of the sample. Firearms (including revolvers, semi-automatic handguns, semi-automatic rifles, and shotguns) were used in 58 percent of the incidents. Additionally, firearms often were involved in incidents where multiple weapons were used.

Figure 2.5
Type of Weapon

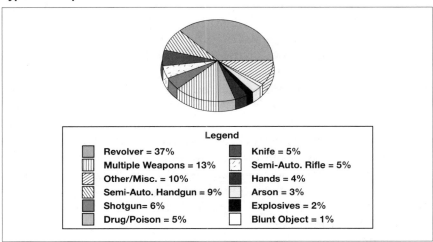

Legend	
Revolver = 37%	Knife = 5%
Multiple Weapons = 13%	Semi-Auto. Rifle = 5%
Other/Misc. = 10%	Hands = 4%
Semi-Auto. Handgun = 9%	Arson = 3%
Shotgun= 6%	Explosives = 2%
Drug/Poison = 5%	Blunt Object = 1%

Source: Compiled by M. Southerland, P. Collins & K. Scarborough.

Love Triangle. Of the 37 incidents involving domestic or intimate partner disputes or romantic rejection, 5 incidents were identified as involving a love triangle based on the information available.

Workplace Violence as Part of Another Crime. Ninety percent of the incidents were committed as single acts, without the involvement of another crime. Twenty-four cases were identified as occurring in conjunction with another crime. Of these, robbery was the most frequently committed (n=19).

Alcohol or Drug Involvement. Drug or alcohol use at the time of the workplace violence incident was indicated in only 10 cases.

Job Action Concurrent with or Immediately Preceding the Incident. Only 14 percent of the incidents were reported as occurring during or immediately following a job action. This low percentage appears to indicate that workplace violence incidents are not as often related to job action (disciplinary action) as has been reported. It does demonstrate that employees do not frequently respond violently at the time of the job action. However, this data, because of the nature of the question, does not capture those cases in which employees returned months or even years after a job action, to commit a violent act in their former place of employment. Several of the cases reported in Chapter 3 reflect such delayed response.

Profile of Violent Offenders

Based on the available data (N=282) the typical offender in the workplace setting can be described as a male U.S. citizen who is 33 years old, a full-time, non-management employee in the site where the workplace violence occurs, is married, has two children, commits the violence alone, is uninjured at the close of the incident, has never been fired from a job, has a good work history, no previous arrests, no psychiatric history, has no record of military service, was not known as a violent person, has never threatened violence in the workplace nor committed previous violence, was not using drugs at the time of the incident, is not feared by others, is not a loner, and was motivated to commit this crime by a perception that the organization or someone in it had wronged him.

Demographics. Ninety-seven percent of all offenders were U.S. citizens. Ninety percent of the offenders were male. The median age of the offenders was 33 (see Figure 2.6), falling in the 26-35 age category.

Figure 2.6
Offenders by Age Category

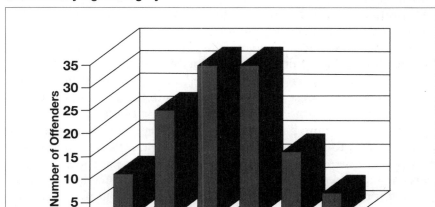

Source: Compiled by M. Southerland, P. Collins & K. Scarborough.

Family. Other studies of workplace violence presented no information about the family situation of the offender. For the vast majority of the offenders in this study, there was little information about their family situation. Children of the offenders were mentioned in only 14 percent of the cases. The median number of children per offender was two.

The offender's marital status was known for 27 percent of them. When it was indicated, the marital status was often relevant to the incident. Of the 76 offenders for which marital status was indicated in the news releases: 43 percent were married, 37 percent were single and the remaining 20 percent were evenly divided between the categories of divorced and separated. Therefore, 63 percent had been married at some point in time.

Race. The race of the offender was known for only nine percent of the cases and was equally distributed between white and non-white categories (4% white; 5% non-white). Race is the only variable of consequence for which less information was available in this database than would be from police reports (for the offender) or death certificates (for the victim). As a variable, race is infrequently report-ed in the printed text of electronic wire services unless it is relevant to the case, i.e., it is part of the motivation for the crime or is part of the justification or defense used in court.

Occupational Type. The specific level of occupational skill could be determined for 62 percent of the offenders. Of them, 42 percent were skilled, 32 percent were unskilled, and 26 percent were white collar employees. These figures do not fit with the general perception of violent crime as a predominantly lower-class phenomenon.

Injury. Sixty-nine percent of the offenders were uninjured at the completion of the violent incident. Twenty percent killed themselves, four percent were killed by police or someone else at the scene, four percent suffered a non-lethal self-inflicted injury, while another three percent were injured by the police or someone else at the scene (see Figure 2.7).

Figure 2.7
Offender's Injury

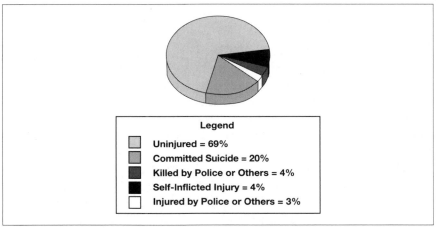

Source: Compiled by M. Southerland, P. Collins & K. Scarborough.

Position in the Organization. Current full-time employees posed the single largest threat for workplace violence. The part-time worker posed a relatively small threat, making up less than five percent of all offenders. Considering only those offenders who were or had been employees of the organization, 67 percent were currently employed by the organization, 24 percent were ex-employees and 10 percent were or had been employed in management-level positions. Seven offenders were owners or presidents of the organization. One was a family member of an employee and another was a union official (one of the murder-for-hire cases). Nineteen percent of all offenders had no work connection to the organization, but were usually one of the multiple offenders who, for this incident, worked with someone who had a workplace connection. A significant percentage of offenders (13%) were customers of the workplace and five percent were romantically involved with an employee of the organization (see Figure 2.8).

Figure 2.8
Offender's Position in Organization

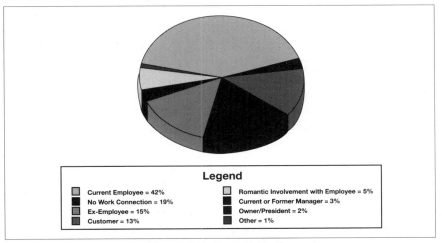

Source: Compiled by M. Southerland, P. Collins & K. Scarborough.

Categories of Offenders

Offenders who commit lethal workplace violence can be categorized as: employees, customers, and intimates of employees. These are the best distinctions for examining motivation of offenders. However, there are two other dimensions that are important. One of these is the factor of suicidal violence versus homicidal violence; some offenders killed themselves while other offenders only killed others. A distinction can also be made between the cases in which the offender survived the incident and those in which the offender died either at the scene of the incident or within days of it, whether as an act of suicide or at the hand of someone else. These two factors should be examined in future research. A brief review of the offender categories follows.

Employees as Offenders. Within the employee category there are two types of offenders who commit workplace violence. One is the former employee who was fired, quit after disciplinary action, quit under threat of being fired, or is on some type of disability from the organization and is dissatisfied with the way the organization has treated them. Twenty percent of all offenders had been fired or were under threat of being fired from the workplace. The other employee category is the current employee (who is often given the label, "disgruntled" by the police, other employees, and the media).

It is important to note here that the employee offender often has a very different perception of reality than management and other employees in the organization. We found it to be a rare case that other employees believed that the offender was being "mistreated" in some way or that other employees thought the offender was so "hurt" by the "mistreatment" that he/she might resort to lethal violence. Such differences in perception are evident in the following case of lethal violence which occurred after our data had been collected.

Constant teasing over a female security officer's weight is believed to have led to lethal violence resulting in the death of the both the female (Rich) who was being teased and the individual responsible for the teasing (Findsen). Both were security guards on the grounds of a Michigan State Police administrative complex in Lansing. The shooting occurred about 3:50 a.m. Friday, January 17, 1997. The guards drew their 9mm automatic handguns and shot each other to death inside the gated grounds of the complex where they worked. Their bodies were found about 25 feet apart, one on each side of their idling patrol car. A wall behind Findsen's body was riddled with bullets. The application for a search warrant of Rich's home indicated that Findsen had been teasing Rich "relentlessly" about her weight. "The teasing had been going on for several months and Rich was angry about it." A longtime friend of Rich said that she was heavy but that she did not seem overly sensitive about her weight (Teasing, 1997:2A).

As with the employee offender, it is also quite likely that the disgruntled customer and intimate of an employee who commits violence in the workplace view their situations very differently than anyone in the organization where they commit their lethal acts.

Customers as Offenders. The offenders who fell in this category were always described as "disgruntled." Their dissatisfaction with the organization resulted from such things as losing a great deal of money on the stock market, dissatisfaction with a product that had been purchased, an administrative mistake that went uncorrected, or "salt inadvertently being rubbed into a sore wound," by the generation of a form letter notifying the customer that he still owed money on a car that had been repossessed.

Intimates of Employees as Offenders. These offenders were generally former lovers or spouses for which there had been a recent argument or breakup. This type of offender is covered in more detail in a later section of this chapter that deals with domestic violence as a special circumstance of workplace violence. Another type of intimate is a "would be" lover who has been rejected and has possibly stalked the employee with whom they would like to have a relationship. The most rare type of intimate offender was the family member of an employee.

Pre-Employment Variables

This section presents the results of our study for those variables that might be indicated on a pre-employment application or reference check. Many of them have been suggested in the literature as important variables for predicting workplace violence.

Previous Arrest. Nine percent of all offenders had a previous arrest record.

Previously Fired. Three percent of all offenders had been fired from past jobs.

Psychiatric History. Six percent of the offenders had a history of mental illness.

Work History. Twelve percent of the offenders had a problematic work history, indicative of potential problems.

Military Background. Much has been made in the workplace violence literature about the military status of the offender. We found this to be an insignificant factor. Four percent of the offenders in our study were still serving in the military. Only two of the 282 offenders had been dishonorably discharged, while three had less than honorable discharges. Together the "dishonorably" discharged, offenders account for less than two percent of the offender population.

Six percent of the offenders had been honorably discharged and nine percent were too young to serve in the military. For the vast majority (83%) of our offenders, there was no indication in the news report of prior service in the military. Based on the tendency of media sources to include information items that have heightened public interest, it is our impression that most of these offenders had no prior military service.

For those offenders for whom their branch of service was noted (total n=24), 13 were Navy, six Army, four Air Force, and one Marine. Based on the previous literature, one would have expected them to have been in the Army or Marines. For those still serving in the Military (n=21), 12 were in the Reserves, five in the National Guard, and four on Active Duty. Only two offenders (.4%) were noted to be prior members of the special forces, yet, heretofore, this was an accepted predisposition that could be found throughout the workplace violence literature.

Only one offender is known to have served in Vietnam. The attention given to the Vietnam experience as a precursor to workplace violence appears unwarranted.

Warning Signs

Several variables examined in this research can be and are often used as indicators of potential workplace violence. The findings demonstrate the potential effectiveness of their use to predict these incidents.

Offender Described as Violent. Only 9 percent of the offenders were described as violent by those who were interviewed or gave statements to the print media reporters.

Offender Previously Threatened Violence. Twenty-seven percent of the offenders had previously threatened violence in the workplace. The difference between the results in this variable and the previous one in which the offender is described as violent is the "threat" versus "observed" violent behavior or the perception that the individual was violent. In many cases where the offender had threatened violence, workers around them discounted the threat. They did not believe the offender would ever carry out the threat.

Offender Committed Previous Violence. Sixteen percent of the offenders were known to have been violent in the past. The previous violence referred to here may have taken place either in or out of the workplace and may have taken place several years earlier. That which took place outside the workplace and several years earlier was often unknown to co-workers and thereby explains some of the difference between the "perceptions" of offenders as violent and the "actual" commission of violence.

Prior Incidents Reported to Management. Prior reports of threats, fear, or actual violence were made to management before this incident for only seven percent of the offenders while such incidents went unreported for 10 percent of the offenders. Thus, only 17 percent of the offenders gave some blatant warning signs of potential violent behavior.

Drugs/Alcohol. Another variable that is often mentioned in the literature and was mentioned earlier in this chapter is the influence of drugs and alcohol on offender behavior. Our research indicates a low involvement of drugs and alcohol in these incidents. Only eight offenders (less than 3%) were reportedly under the influence of drugs and/or alcohol at the time of the incident. The typical offender has the full use of his mental abilities and makes a determined choice to commit this violence.

Feared by Others. Engendering fear in others has also been alluded to in the literature as a factor in workplace violence. For our study it was reported for only nine percent of the offenders.

Loner. This variable is mentioned in almost all the workplace violence literature. Only 12 offenders (4%) in our study were referred to in ways that they might be considered loners.

Motivating Factors

There were six common motives for the offender to commit workplace violence:

1. disgruntled employee (17% of offenders)

2. domestic violence (13% of offenders)

3. robbery (12% of offenders)

4. fired employee/employee in fear of being fired (10% of offenders)

5. disgruntled customer (9% of offenders)

6. on-strike employee/picket-line violence (3% of offenders)

When all the individual motive categories with a frequency of less than 1.5 percent were added together, they accounted for a total of 20 percent of all offenders. The motive could not be determined for 16 percent of the offenders. Figure 2.9 presents the known motivation for the primary offender in each incident grouped by the major categories into which they fall.

Figure 2.9
Offender's Motivation

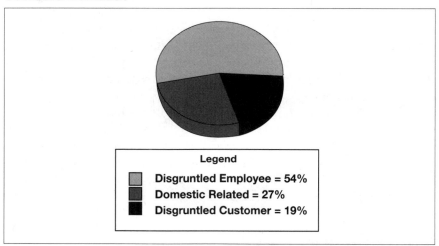

Source: Compiled by M. Southerland, P. Collins & K. Scarborough.

Motivation by Offender's Age. Offender motives were significantly different when examined by age category. Juvenile offenders had not been fired from previous jobs while adults 19 to 45 years of age were more likely to be motivated due to a firing incident, potential or past. Juveniles were more likely to be disgruntled *customers* than their adult counterparts. Offenders from 26 to 55 years of age were more likely to be disgruntled *employees*. Domestic violence was a more prevalent motivation for offenders 19 to 45 years of age while it was almost non-existent in the other age categories.

Motivation by Other Variables. There was no significant difference found when the motivation of offenders was compared by any of the following variables: the *site,* the degree of *injury* inflicted on the offender at the close of the incident, the *criminal justice status* of the case, the *charge,* the *sentence,* and the *year* the incident occurred.

The decision to commit workplace violence is a rational one in which the offender decides to use lethal violence to cope with stress, to get even, to reassert his/her superiority, or in retaliation for real or perceived mistreatment.

Women as Offenders

In their review of the research on the homicidal behavior of women, Ogle, Maier-Katin, and Bernard (1995) note findings that 80 percent of homicides committed by women involve the killing of an intimate. They often kill as a result of a long-term abusive relationship, they generally kill in the home, and their homicides are generally spontaneous. The female offenders in our study contradict these findings in the following ways: all the homicides were committed outside the home in a workplace setting, they were planned, and they were not targeting an abusive partner.

Ogle, et al. (1995) present a new theory of homicidal behavior among women. This theory was designed to explain women's homicidal behavior in all of the settings in which it might occur. In this theory they state the following propositions:

1. Women experience higher stress than men.

2. Women of lower social status experience higher stress than those who have higher social status.

3. Women have more blockages on anger coping mechanisms than men.

4. Women of lower social status experience more blockages on anger coping mechanisms than those who have higher social status.

5. Women are more likely than men to develop overcontrolling personalities.

6. "Women are less likely than men to have developed regulative rules for the experience and expression of anger." (1995:186)

7. Women are more likely than men to explode in an episode of extreme uncontrolled violence when experiencing high stress.

8. "Targets of this violence are most likely to be those in the immediate environment, whether or not those targets represent the actual source of stress." (1995:186)

This theory does not appear to be applicable to the incidents of lethal violence in the workplace. Our data show that women are rarely offenders in workplace violence cases. Nevertheless, when women commit workplace violence, they have the same types of *motives* as men. Female offenders are more likely to leave the scene of workplace violence unharmed than their male counterparts. Only 12 percent of women kill themselves, compared to 20 percent of men, and none are killed or injured by someone else. Women were effective in their attempts to commit suicide, none were left with self-inflicted injuries.

Fifty percent of the female offenders were employees compared to 39 percent of men. Women offenders were less likely than their male counterparts to be customers and less likely to be romantically involved with an employee.

There was a significant difference between the gender of offenders when the criminal justice status of the case was examined. There was also a significant difference by gender for the criminal charge and the number of years the offender was sentenced to prison. In cases of workplace violence, women (54%) were more likely than men (36%) to be charged with murder. Women received shorter prison sentences than men. The sentences for women ranged from a low of 10 years to a high of 18 years while sentences for males ranged from a low of one year to a high of 261 years.

Female offenders were, statistically, significantly younger than their male counterparts with the median age for women being 30 and the median age for men being 36.

Women have not received the death penalty nor have they been executed for offenses related to workplace violence. A higher percentage of women had been charged or arrested (58%) and were awaiting trial than men (45%).

Criminal Justice System Response to Offenders

The Offender is Typically Apprehended at the Scene. Generally, the offender is either dead or surrenders to police. These offenders are rarely killed by police. Those who die take the motivation to the grave with them. They rarely leave a suicide note and searches of their homes and computer files uncover no clues regarding the stimulus for their violent incident.

Apprehension. Ninety-seven percent of offenders had been apprehended by police. This represents a much larger percentage of immediate apprehensions than is generally true for lethal violence. The apprehension rate is particularly different from that of serial murderers in general who kill multiple times before being caught. Levin and Fox (1985) found this same distinction between serial and simultaneous mass killers. Their research found simultaneous killings were solved with comparative ease and the perpetrators were caught quickly while serial murders were far more elusive. In the case of workplace violence, the offender is often known to the survivors who are employed in the workplace because this individual is or has been a co-worker, a known customer, or a known intimate of a co-worker.

The Offender Also Rarely Escapes the Scene Without Being Caught. One of the similarities between the simultaneous workplace violence incident and incidents of mass murder both simultaneous and serial is the fact that in most cases everyone involved is shocked that this person did it. The workplace violence offender is a normal person with no prior threats and the violence was not anticipated, furthermore, people who knew the offender well indicated disbelief that this individual was capable of such a violent act. Often they indicated that they knew the offender's circumstances were bad but they did not think this individual could be driven to kill.

The Charge. Of the 214 offenders who did not die at the scene and were apprehended by the police, 46 percent were charged with murder, one percent with negligent homicide, twelve percent with assault, and 14 percent with some other charge. The charge was unknown or not reported for 27 percent of the offenders in the electronic news reports of AP and UPI during the time frame accessed for our study. For purposes of this study we coded the charge as the highest charge of those made by criminal justice agencies.

Status of Case. Forty-nine percent of all offenders were in the very early stages of the criminal justice process, having been arrested and in jail or released on bond. Two of the offenders had been executed. Another six were on death row. One had been paroled and later committed suicide, most likely as a result of his alienation from society and the public outcry against his return to the "outside."

Only Two Offenders Received a Probation Sentence. An additional 12 percent of offenders were serving their prison sentence. The median prison sentence received was 30 years; the shortest was one year and the longest was 261 years.

Profile of Victims

The typical victim of workplace violence is a 42-year-old male full-time employee in a non-managerial position in a service industry organization. He died as a result of a gunshot wound. Very rarely was the race/ethnicity or marital status of the victim given in the AP or UPI news reports. Marital status could only be determined for 11 percent of the victims and was usually determined by statements concerning the relationship between the victim and the offender or by a statement made by a victim's spouse. Marital status was apparent (single) for young children who were victimized, and therefore is known. Due to the nature of national print media, we know most about those who are killed, less about the injured, and have almost no information about those threatened but unharmed. One of the significant differences in serial mass murder as reported by Levin and Fox (1985) and our findings in workplace violence is that the number of victims is a known quantity in workplace violence while the total number of victims of a serial murderer may never be known.

Gender. For those victims for whom gender was known, 62 percent were female and 38 percent were male. There was a significant difference in the injury suffered by gender. Female victims were more likely to be threatened or killed while male victims were more likely to be injured.

Age. The mean reported age of the victims was 42.

Figure 2.10
Victims by Age Category

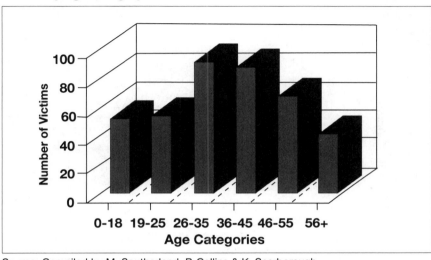

Source: Compiled by M. Southerland, P. Collins & K. Scarborough.

Family. Family information is unavailable for most victims. This type of data is not available at all in other research on workplace violence. The available data reflect that the median number of children for victims is one; 60 percent of the victims were married, 35 percent were single, and six percent were either separated or divorced. Two victims were pregnant at the time of the workplace violence incident.

Numbers of Victims. There were 935 victims in the incidents we examined. Figure 2.11 shows the numbers of victims by year. Reports of victims before 1983 are incomplete due to the AP and UPI databases beginning in 1983. As discussed earlier, victimizations reported before 1983 are due to later news reports of the status of a criminal case or a civil suit against the estate of the assailant. When examining trends in victimizations, 1983 should be the starting point.

Degree of Injury

Of 935 victims, 42 percent were killed, 35 percent were injured (24% of those being seriously injured), and 22 percent were under serious threat of lethal violence (see Figure 2.12). In cases where serious threat occurred, the typical scenario was that individuals were taken hostage or were under fire.

Figure 2.11
Victims by Year

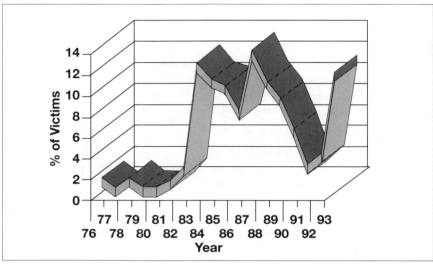

Source: Compiled by M. Southerland, P. Collins & K. Scarborough.

Figure 2.12
Victim's Injury

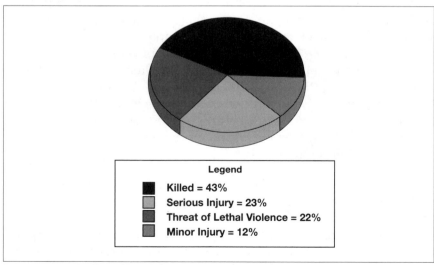

Source: Compiled by M. Southerland, P. Collins & K. Scarborough.

Total Killed. There was a total of 532 people killed in all 246 incidents of workplace violence. The number of people killed in any single incident ranged from 1 to 42. Those incidents in which only one person was killed, constituted 31 percent of the total, while incidents in which two persons were killed represented 11 percent. Of those killed, 491 (96%) were killed in the workplace. Those killed outside a workplace reflect the incidents which were multiple site incidents.

Multiple Site. Only four percent of all workplace violence victims were killed outside the workplace in multiple site events. Multiple site cases are extremely rare events, but when there are multiple sites, the case usually involves the killing and injury of family members or others who have an intimate relationship with the offender. Of these multiple-site victims, 23 were killed at their residence, 32 were killed in a public place, and 28 were killed at an isolated location.

Total Injured. A total of 404 persons were injured in the 246 workplace violence incidents. In 47 percent of the incidents there were no physical injuries, but threats only (see Figure 2.12 for the level of injury by victim). The range of injuries per incident was 1 to 57. Those incidents having a single person injured account for 22 percent of the sample, while incidents involving only two injured persons constitute 16 percent of the sample. The significance of this statistic is the "innocent bystander" effect. In addition to those individuals who may be direct targets (intended victims), many others fall victim to these attacks.

Types of Victims

Position in the Organization. Figure 2.12 shows the relative organizational position of the victims. The single largest percentage of the victims were employees (39%). Customers made up the second highest category (23%) of victims. Customers would not typically have been considered part of the organization until Total Quality Management came into vogue. Because the organization has a responsibility to provide a safe climate not only for employees but for their customers, the customers are included here. Managers and owners or presidents of the company made up another 14 percent of the victims. Security personnel and police officers each made up one percent of the victim pool. Most of the police were victimized as a result of responding to a scene of lethal workplace violence. There were no cases, during the time frame examined, in which a police officer was killed or injured as a result of the violent act of someone with a direct relationship to the police organization.

Figure 2.13
Victim's Organizational Position

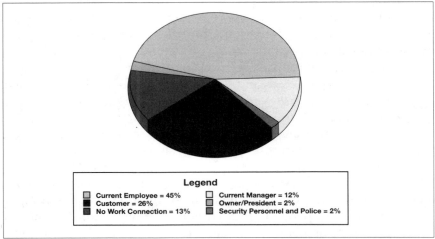

Legend	
☐ Current Employee = 45%	☐ Current Manager = 12%
■ Customer = 26%	☐ Owner/President = 2%
■ No Work Connection = 13%	■ Security Personnel and Police = 2%

Source: Compiled by M. Southerland, P. Collins & K. Scarborough.

A new case that illustrates the paucity of information that is frequently given about victims follows: Three security officers were seriously injured by gunshot on Thursday, May 19, 1995, at Opryland's residence hotel for immigrant workers. The suspect, Adrian Maldorado, an immigrant worker, entered the office about 10:20 p.m. and told an officer he was sick. When the officer examined Maldorado, the suspect grabbed the guard's weapon and started shooting. The suspect was to be charged with aggravated assault (Opryland, 1995). A possible way to gain more information about victims who were killed would be through obituaries. For those who are injured, police reports and local newspaper coverage might provide additional information. However, such examinations are beyond the scope of this work and will be left to future endeavors on this topic. This research has given considerably more detailed information regarding offenders and victims than has been available in previous studies of workplace violence.

Site of Victimization

The largest number of victims (16%) were victimized in a restaurant. The second most common site of victimization was office buildings (12%). This finding is reversed from the results for incidents. The explanation is simple: more individuals were victimized in the incidents of workplace violence in restaurants while incidents which occurred in office buildings had fewer victims.

Tied for third in the number of victimizations were plants and manufacturing sites with 10 percent and medical sites with 10 percent. Hotels were fourth with eight percent (primarily due to a single incident) while airlines came in fifth with six percent. The single most well-publicized site of lethal workplace violence, the U.S. post office, accounted for only six percent of the victimizations. Schools were next with five percent, then retail sales with four percent. Home or apartment buildings made up four percent of the victimizations. Other government agencies accounted for four percent, while the recreation and entertainment industry accounted for three percent of the victimizations. Other sites individually made up less than two percent but together accounted for nine percent of the victimizations. The remaining sites were unknown. Figure 2.13 presents the victimizations grouped by type of site.

Figure 2.14
Victimizations by Type of Site

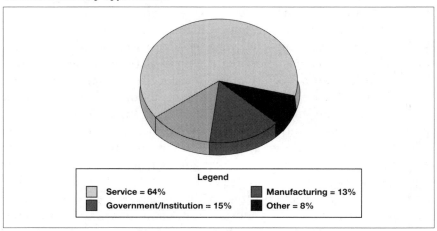

Source: Compiled by M. Southerland, P. Collins & K. Scarborough.

It is apparent from this data that the service industry accounts for the most substantial portion of victimizations in lethal workplace violence. If they are all added together, victimizations that occur in a site where the business provides a direct service to the public, comprise nearly 80 percent of all victimizations.

The Victim's Role in Triggering Violence

The victim had no role in precipitating the conflict in 80 percent of the cases. Three percent of the victims had refused the romantic advances of the assailant on some previous occasion. Four percent of the victims had been involved with firing, disciplining, or otherwise counseling the assailant to change his behavior. Three percent of the victims had argued with or had a property dispute with the victim. Some other disagreement or conflict occurred in 10 percent of the cases.

The Victim-Offender Relationship

Work Relationship. A surprising 52 percent of the victims of lethal workplace violence had no work relationship to the assailant. The next highest single relationship was that of co-workers being victimized (19%). When former co-workers are added in, the percent in this category increases to 24 percent.

Immediate Supervisors Made Up Only Four Percent of the Victims. When former immediate supervisors are included the percentage increases to six percent. Subordinates were the smallest group of victims, making up only one percent of the victim pool. Two very unusual victims were a co-owner and an ex-partner of the assailant.

Intimate Relationship. The vast majority of the victims (88%) had no intimate relationship with the assailant. Of the remaining victims, two percent were either the current spouse, live-in lover, or dating partner of the assailant; two percent were the ex-spouse, ex-lover, or ex-dating partner of the assailant; and one percent rejected the assailant's attention after being sought as a lover. Interestingly, an equal percentage of victims were considered "friends of the assailant" and were "sought as lovers." If intimate categories are examined solely, more of the assailants' children (1.3%) and other family members (1.3%) were victims than any other single category except for the category of spouse (1.6%). The children and other family members were typically killed in a setting apart from the workplace in multi-site incidents of lethal violence. Only one victim was the rival for the attention of the assailant's love interest while there were five incidents which involved a love triangle.

Domestic Violence as a Special Case

Domestic violence is the violence that occurs between intimates. It may occur between spouses or dating partners. Some include general family violence in this category. The significance of the problem of domestic violence and the response that should be made to it has been well documented elsewhere (see Buzawa & Buzawa, 1990; Fagan, 1989; Gelles, 1987; Ohlin & Tonry, 1989; Pagelow, 1989; and Sigler, 1989).

The Nature of Domestic Violence in the Workplace. There are four primary types of lethal domestic violence incidents in the workplace. One is that of a husband, estranged husband, or ex-husband intending to harm his wife, estranged wife, or ex-wife. The second is the boyfriend or ex-boyfriend intending to harm his girlfriend or ex-girlfriend. The third is a would-be boyfriend who has been rejected and enters the workplace to harm the woman who rejected him. This third type frequently has stalked the intended girlfriend and she may have obtained a restraining order against him. The fourth type is different because the intended victim is the individual whom the offender holds responsible for the "broken" relationship between him and the object of his affection. The typical lethal domestic violence incident in the workplace fits one of the first three types, the husband or male companion commits a violent act with the intention of harming his wife or female companion. The high percentage of males as offenders compared to females as offenders in workplace violence incidents contrasts with the findings of Wilson and Daly (1992) regarding spousal homicide. Wilson and Daly found that for every 100 U.S. men who kill their wives, 75 women kill their husbands. Our data revealed a distinctly different ratio. For every 34 men who commit lethal domestic violence in the workplace, only two women commit that same crime. There were 37 cases in this data that had domestic violence as a motive. Most of the multi-site cases included domestic violence but the motive was coded for the workplace violence; therefore, those cases are not included here. The highest percentage of domestic violence offenders were in the 26- to 35-year age range.

Year. The incidents of workplace domestic violence peaked in three years: 1984 (16%), 1986 (14%), and 1987 (16%).

Site. Domestic violence occurred predominantly in service sites (59%).

Offender's Relationship to the Organization. Domestic violence offenders either had no work relationship to the organization (32%), were employees (30%), were romantically involved with an employee of the organization (27%), or were a customer of the organization (8%). No managerial employee committed domestic violence.

Offender's Injury. Offenders in workplace domestic violence cases usually escaped without injury (60%), while nine killed themselves (24%) and two were killed by police or others (5%).

Criminal Charge. The workplace domestic violence offender was charged with murder most frequently (29%). Seventeen percent of these offenders were charged with assault or some other charge. Another 29 percent died; therefore, a charge was not applicable.

Impact on the Workplace

Unintended Victims. All too frequently with domestic violence and other types of workplace violence cases the victims are not those who were the original target of the offender. They are truly innocent bystanders. The offender selects the time and means but often is not in control of who happens to be in the workplace at the chosen time. It is fairly common that the intended victim escapes harm while others are killed. The tragedy has lasting psychological repercussions on all who "experience" it.

Psychological Consequences. One of the biggest effects of domestic violence cases is the inability of co-workers to protect their friends who are victims of domestic violence. This feeling of helplessness can cause lost productivity in the workplace for months if there is no aftercare for victims and their families.

Practice Exercise for Chapter 2

The intent of the practice exercises is to encourage the reader to use critical thinking skills in planning for and possibly preventing incidents of workplace violence. Often there are no right or wrong answers because each situation is different depending on the workplace setting and the individuals involved. The reader has different levels of information available as he/she proceeds through the text; however, each exercise should be attempted given the current information available. After reading the remainder of the text, the reader might choose to come back to earlier exercises and examine the answers to see if he/she would change them in light of added information.

The following exercise focuses on the behaviors of a particular employee who has been fired and asks the reader to identify warning indicators of the incident and to determine what actions might be taken to prevent the incident.

The Case of the Fired Employee

Paul Calden was a 33-year-old former insurance manager for Fireman's Fund Insurance Company, Tampa, Florida. On November 27, 1993, he entered the cafeteria of the company where he had been employed for two years and proceeded to a table where five of his former bosses were eating, and shot at them with a handgun. Three people were killed and two seriously injured. Police thought he might have remained in the 12-story building so they performed a search and found that he had changed clothes and fled the scene before killing himself 15 miles away. He left no clues regarding the incident. A review of hundreds of personal computer disks in his apartment revealed nothing to help the homicide investigation. The lead police investigator said, "We can only believe he was severely disgruntled and never forgave them for firing him."

Calden had a history of making threats against colleagues and nearly had a fist fight with a supervisor before being fired eight months before this incident. When he was let go after two years of employment, he left with the statement, "You haven't seen the last of me."

Examples of incidents in Calden's record:

- He filed a harassment complaint after a co-worker displayed a bumper sticker that mentioned "kicking a Gator." Calden considered it offensive to his alma mater.

- He came close to having a fist fight with a supervisor over a written reprimand. Another supervisor intervened to prevent punches from being thrown.

- He threatened to sue the Fireman's Fund Insurance Company for denying him a merit raise.

- He blamed the company for bleeding ulcers that he claimed he suffered from, and said that as a result, he demanded regular blood transfusions to replace the loss of one pint of blood per day. When supervisors asked him to provide documentation of his illness, he refused. The autopsy performed after his death revealed no ulcers.

- He threatened a female co-worker who had parked in his favorite parking spot. He denied reports that he had cursed at her and that he had threatened to sue her.

- Supervisors had enough. They decided to fire him for misconduct, alleging he lied about his illness to receive paid time off from work.

Your Task

1. First, consider this case in specific. List the factors that give you reason to believe that this individual might commit a lethal workplace violence incident.

_____

_____

_____

_____

_____

2. What actions do you think should have been taken by management and employees in this incident?

_____

_____

_____

_____

_____

_____

3. If a person in *your* organization were to exhibit the same behaviors as Calden:

   a. How would employees in *your* organization respond?

   _____

   _____

   _____

   _____

   b. How would management in *your* organization respond?

   _____

   _____

   _____

   _____

c. What should employees in *your* organization do to effectively respond to this situation? How does this response differ from that in question 2 above? Why?

_____

_____

_____

_____

_____

_____

_____

_____

d. What should management in *your* organization do to effectively respond to this situation? How does this response differ from that in question 2 above? Why?

_____

_____

_____

_____

_____

_____

_____

3   Incidents of Workplace Violence

This chapter presents illustrative case examples of workplace violence incidents. The intention is to provide a set of cases depicting the diverse nature of workplace violence. An attempt has been made to select cases based on their relative proportions within the data. However, for certain types, we presented additional cases to provide the reader with more complete information and a better understanding of the phenomenon. The typology presented in Chapter 2 is used to organize the cases. Employees have been separated into current and former employees for clarity.

Employee Violence in Service Organizations

Current Employees

* Robert D'Agostino, a 30-year-old restaurant employee was charged with assault and battery and damage to personal property when he allegedly punched a customer, doused another one with hot wax, and pulled off their tablecloth. The unidentified elderly couple had asked for extra condiments and D'Agostino went to speak to the couple about their request. Prior to D'Agostino taking physical action, a shouting match

between the male customer and the offender occurred. After the incident indoors, the offender smashed the couple's car windshield which was parked outside of the restaurant. Other restaurant employees would not comment on the incident.

- On February 22, 1984, Wesley Toole, 45, a railroad employee in Los Angeles, held a railroad executive hostage after dousing him with gasoline. Toole threatened to set the hostage ablaze unless Toole was paid $15 million and given back his old job. Toole had worked for the company since 1965 as a railroad brakeman, before taking a medical leave for more than one year due to a history of mental problems. Police said Toole, carrying an attaché case and two gallons of gasoline, splashed fuel on two employees before grabbing the hostage and dragging him into an office. Although a security guard fired one shot, no one was hit or injured. Toole wanted the money to compensate for his discomfort from a lack of fair treatment during his past employment. At the end of a three hour stand-off with police, SWAT officers rushed into the office and apprehended Toole. The hostage had suffered some minor injury and was listed in satisfactory condition.

- On Saturday morning, February 6, 1993, Fernando Ruiz, who worked in retail sales, was called into his boss's office and told he was being fired for theft and harassment of a female employee. Ruiz went to his car and returned with a semi-automatic pistol and shot his boss, 30-year-old Richard Dahn, several times in the upper body. He then walked to the back office area and shot a female co-worker several times. Next, Dahn climbed into the attic and shot himself in the head. Ruiz and Dahn were pronounced dead at the scene. The female co-worker underwent surgery and was listed in critical condition.

- Nelson Sergio, 19, was upset about not getting a promotion. On October 4, 1993, he shot and killed two co-workers as they sat in their car outside the Target department store where all three worked. One of the victims had been the recipient of the promotion.

- Following a promotional dispute in April 1987, a 31-year-old female accounting representative walked into her office, shot her boss and another manager with a .38 caliber revolver and then shot herself. The woman had been with the accounting firm since 1979 and was supposedly upset because she had not received a promotion. There were no reports that the woman had threatened her employers but several of her co-workers "noticed her dissatisfaction about things happening at work." The offender shot herself fatally, and the two victims survived, both with serious injuries.

- On February 23, 1994, five current and former casino workers robbed the Merv Griffin Resorts Casino Hotel in Atlantic City, New Jersey, taking more than $1 million. A 57-year-old female unarmed security guard was shot in the eye and neck, causing her to lose vision in one eye. A discarded ID badge, security video tape, and the fact that one member of the ring went to the police to report that the getaway car had been stolen helped police solve the case and capture the workers within 24 hours. The names of the five employees had not been released.

- An 18-year-old Wendy's restaurant employee in Ft. Lauderdale, Florida, allegedly shot and killed his boss and two co-workers during a robbery attempt of the restaurant. Bernell Hegwood told police that he had only intended to rob the restaurant, but that he had to shoot the workers when "his body was taken over by the spirit of a Louisiana murderer." Hegwood indicated that he had been overcome by the spirit of a convicted cop killer on death row in Louisiana, who was also his mother's boyfriend. According to the offender, he had been in the restroom with another employee "fooling around" with a .32 caliber pistol when the gun discharged, killing the other employee. He further indicated that he had decided that he would then have to kill the manager and other employee who was on duty at the time. Although Hegwood escaped with $1,700 in cash and several boxes of frozen ground beef patties, he was later captured by police following a tip from his mother.

- Andrew Eggleston was a 35-year-old sales manager at a car dealership in Rochester, New York. On February 18, 1985, Eggleston rigged an M-80 firecracker inside a company car of a salesperson, the explosion ruptured an eardrum, broke seven bones in the victim's left hand, and caused him to lose the tips of three fingers. Eggleston claimed his actions were meant as a prank. He was charged with unlawfully dealing with fireworks, punishable by a fine.

- John Lee Swanay was a 60-year-old co-owner of the Painted Lady restaurant in Kansas City, Missouri. There was a dispute with his co-owner over the placement of a couch in the restaurant. On January 6, 1985, Swanay shot and killed his co-owner as she exited her vehicle. He then proceeded to fire at the woman's husband as he ran away. Swanay followed, but was tackled by his male lover, an employee of the restaurant. The lover shot and killed Swanay and then killed himself. An innocent bystander was also wounded.

- The most unusual case of this type occurred on July 27, 1993. Ramona Johnson, a 22-year-old supervisor in an Indianapolis Taco Bell restaurant, ordered an employee, Anthony Price, 28, to give a gun to Darnell Johnson, 18, who was a customer in the restaurant. Ramona Johnson then yelled for Darnell to shoot Jerry Emmert, another customer in the drive-thru lane. Darnell Johnson fatally shot Emmert once in the chest and three times in the back.

    Emmert and five friends had been out drinking, traveling in a rented limousine, when they decided to stop for food at Taco Bell. Darnell Johnson was in the drive-thru lane behind Emmert. Johnson's stereo was playing very loudly. Emmert got out of the limousine and complained to Johnson that Johnson's stereo was so loud he was having trouble ordering. Emmert had no weapon and the Deputy County Prosecutor indicated there was no evidence that Emmert was threatening anyone. It was then that Ramona Johnson allegedly ordered Anthony Price, to take a handgun she had sold to him several weeks earlier out to Darnell Johnson, which Price did. Ramona Johnson then yelled out the window for Darnell Johnson to shoot

Emmert. He shot Emmert once in the chest and three times in the back. Darnell Johnson told police he fired the gun in self-defense because he felt threatened by Emmert.

Ramona Johnson, the instigator of this incident, was charged with murder and held under a $500,000 bond. Darnell Johnson, the "trigger man," was also charged with murder and held without bond. Anthony Price was charged with criminal recklessness and assisting a criminal. Ramona and Darnell Johnson are not related.

Former Employees

- Michael George Michaels was a 31-year-old former sales manager for Rite-o-Way in Los Angeles, California. On January 24, 1984, Michaels sent a bomb to Joshua Brown, President of Rite-o-Way, which resulted in serious injury to Brown. The bombing incident was in retaliation for a business dispute between the two individuals. Michaels was sentenced to 30 years in prison.

- David Burke had been employed by USAir for 14 years, before he was fired from the airline. On December 7, 1987, Burke smuggled a .44 caliber handgun onto a commercial airline flight en route to San Francisco from Los Angeles. The cockpit recorder picked up six shots. The plane crashed, killing all 43 people on board. Burke had blamed one of the victims of the crash for his firing.

- Rudy Bladel, a disgruntled former railroad employee, confessed to killing three railroad employees on December 31, 1978, at an Amtrack station in Jackson, Michigan, and was convicted and sentenced to three concurrent life terms. Bladel was not arrested as a suspect in the crime until the 12-gauge shotgun allegedly used in the murders was found a few months after the crime. Bladel had purchased the shotgun two years previously in Indiana. He was arrested in Eckhart, Indiana, on March 22, 1979, (three months after the shooting) and was extradited to Michigan. At a state court arraignment the day after his extradition to Jackson, Michigan, Bladel requested a court-appointed attorney. Three days later, two Jackson police officers visited Bladel at the county jail and questioned him after he had waived his right to remain silent and to be represented by a lawyer during the questioning. During that session he confessed to the murders. The confession was used as evidence in the trial, which resulted in the conviction and three concurrent life sentences. The state Supreme Court threw out the conviction on December 28, 1984, ruling that the confession should not have been admitted as evidence. The U.S. Supreme Court agreed to consider reinstating the murder conviction on May 28, 1985.

• On August 18, 1992, Donald Eugene Daniels, a 21-year-old former employee of Lee's Famous Recipe restaurant in Tulsa, Oklahoma, went to the restaurant to commit a robbery. He forced four employees into the refrigerator, onto their knees, and proceeded to shoot each one in the head, killing all four. He was arrested and charged with four counts of murder and one count of armed robbery.

Employee Violence in Government/Institutions

Current Employees

• O.C. "Chick" Fero was a teacher at Tohatchi High School in Gallup County, New Mexico. He retaliated for receiving a bad evaluation by entering the Office of the Superintendent of Schools in Truth or Consequences, New Mexico, and firing five shots that killed the Superintendent. Fero then calmly walked out of the office and told the receptionist to call police.

• On March 6, 1985, shortly after reporting for his shift, Steven Brownlee, a 30- year-old postal clerk and 12-year veteran employee of the postal service, opened fire in a mail sorting area of the Atlanta Post Office. Two co-workers were killed and a third, who appeared to be an innocent bystander, was wounded before a co-worker grabbed the gun from him and led other postal employees to safety. Brownlee worked in the mail sorter unit and had no apparent motive for the shootings. There was some exchange of words before the shooting about someone Brownlee knew who had been killed in another county. Some of those working in the area were wearing black in mourning for another co-worker (35-year-old female) whose husband has been charged with her strangulation murder in their suburban home last week. One co-worker reported that Brownlee had been "mentally disturbed for quite some time. He was always talking to himself, always acting abnormal. He wore a Sony Walkman and he'd take the headphones off and he'd just keep on talking. Sometimes he would laugh."

Brownlee was taken into custody at the scene and charged with murder and two counts of aggravated assault. He was taken to the psychiatric unit of a local hospital for evaluation following the incident and later pled insanity. The .22 caliber handgun was recovered. Four shots had been fired and one bullet was left in the chamber.

The victims were a 42-year-old male postal worker who was wounded. A 32-year-old male who had been a postal employee for eight years was killed. A 45-year-old male postal supervisor was killed.

- On June 4, 1993, Tinesha James, a 22-year-old clerk in the probation department of Newark, New Jersey, smuggled a gun to drug enforcer, Al-Damanay Kamau, 25, (AKA: Eddie Lee Oliver Philson) who was waiting outside a courtroom. Kamau fatally shot John Sczyrek, narcotics officer, before he could testify in court. A sheriff's deputy was also wounded.

  James switched jackets with the gunman outside the courthouse and put the "high-powered" handgun in her waistband. She went through the employees' entrance, which allowed her to by-pass metal detectors, and switched jackets again with Kamau outside the courtroom. Kamau approached 30-year-old Sczyrek in the hallway, shot him in the head and wounded a 24-year-old male sheriff's deputy as he fled.

  Kamau was arrested a few blocks away. He was an enforcer of a small drug operation that extended to North Carolina. The motive for this conspiracy to commit murder was to keep a police officer from testifying against Kamau's cousins and James' boyfriend in a drug trial. Both offenders were charged with murder. More arrests were expected. Both were scheduled for court appearances on June 4, 1993.

This courthouse is New Jersey's busiest. Metal detectors and X-ray machines were installed three months earlier on four major entrances but six other entrances used by jurors and county employees with identification were guarded only by sheriff's deputies.

- On August 10, 1985, a 28-year-old engineering student allegedly raped and strangled a 50-year-old secretary. The victim's body was found after she failed to return to her office after lunch. Student witnesses stated that they had looked in the door window of an otherwise empty classroom during the lunch hour and had seen a couple having "some afternoon whoopee," so they did not notify anyone of the circumstances. The offender's mother stated that on the afternoon of the incident, her son had come home in a good mood. Additionally, she described her son as a loner, more interested in getting his computer engineering degree than in socializing with friends or dating.

- After a United States Postal worker was given a letter of suspension, he closed the door of his supervisor's office, punched the supervisor in the face and banged his head on the floor, leaving him unconscious. Twenty-nine-year-old Jerry Lee Roach of Arlington, Texas, then returned to his work station. His co-workers later found the supervisor unconscious in his office. Roach was released on bond and charged with assault. He was being suspended for "attendance deficiencies," usually ranging from 7 to 14 days. The assistant manager of the postal facility indicated that Roach would probably be fired because "it has been a long-standing policy of the postal service (to fire employees) for fighting or threatening anyone."

- On July 12, 1976, Edward Allaway, a janitor at the Cal State Fullerton campus, walked into the library with a .22 caliber rifle and shot nine co-workers at close range. Only two of the victims survived. Allaway was found innocent by reason of insanity for the killings and has been confined at Atascadero State Hospital near San Luis Obispo.

- Not a regular employee but a volunteer, Louis Walker, was a 51-year-old man who collected food for charitable organizations. On April 10, 1992, he was on a loading dock in Pasco, Washington, collecting day-old bread. Walker and a volunteer for another organization argued about who would get the day-old bread for their organization when the victim, an 81-year-old man, struck Walker in the face. Walker then shoved the victim, pushing him off the dock. The victim hit his head and never regained consciousness.

Former Employees

- Wanda Rodgers was a 43-year-old former social worker for the Department of Children's Services in Santa Fe Springs, California. She was upset about being fired more than one year earlier due to poor performance. On February 2, 1993, she walked into her former place of employment and shot her boss in the head with a handgun. An hour later she turned herself in to the Sheriff's department.

- A 47-year-old former telephone company employee, Tony Apodaca, angry over the loss of retirement benefits, took hostages and destroyed more than $10 million of equipment with a gun and cut phone services to 15,000 people. Phone company workers indicated that the offender knew exactly what equipment to use to disable the services. All of the hostages escaped and no one was injured. Apodaca told hostage negotiators that he was "disgruntled over some portion of the benefits of his retirement system," and that he wanted to speak with a "big wheel." He had not previously complained about any of his benefits or threatened anyone at Pacific Bell.

- On October 12, 1991, Joseph Harris, a 35-year-old former mail clerk went to the home of his former supervisor and slashed her to death with a Samurai sword, shot and killed her fiancé, and then went to the post office where he killed two male former co-workers aged 59 and 63. He then threw explosives at police before surrendering. He was heavily armed with a variety of weapons, including hand grenades and an Uzi machine gun, and had left his apartment booby-trapped before starting his violent episode.

The supervisor had filed a harassment complaint against him a year earlier. Two months after Harris was fired from the post office in April 1990, the supervisor filed a complaint with the police alleging that Harris had threatened her on the job. She later decided not to press charges. Harris had been a postal employee since 1981 and had been reprimanded in 1984 for harassing other employees. Harris had no police record other than one speeding ticket. He was known to be a Navy veteran, honorably discharged, who wore fatigues and a black beret. Perceptions of Harris differed. Some described him as "quiet," others said he sometimes "exploded in anger." Former co-workers said, "We were all afraid of him. When he didn't get his way, he would scream and make threats." "It wasn't just her [the supervisor who was killed]. He had problems with all the supervisors. He just blamed her because she made the complaint." Another clerk indicated that he had argued with Harris. "Black, white, female, male, you as well as me. He just disliked people."

Another side of him was known by the superintendent of the apartment building where Harris' mother lived. She said, "He took real good care of his mom. He wasn't one of those loud, off-beat type of guys. He was really nice."

Employee Violence in Manufacturing Organizations

Current Employees:

- On October 14, 1993, Geraldo Manso, a 41-year-old afternoon shift supervisor for a warehouse in Miami, Florida, opened fire, killing one man and injuring two other men. Manso fired at the employees as he shot down from the top of the warehouse while they returned from work-related training. Apparently, Manso was upset because the promotion he had wanted was given to two younger employees whom he had trained. The two injured victims were the younger employees who received the promotions Manso wanted. The victim who died was an unintended victim who was known as Manso's friend.

- Elizabeth Teague was a disgruntled 30-year-old employee of Everready Battery Company in Bennington, Virginia. On October 25, 1991, she shot four supervisors at the plant. Authorities said she set a small fire at the plant around 2 p.m. and then took a gun and shot the supervisors, three men and a woman. The fire was later doused without causing much damage. One of the men was in critical condition, one in guarded but stable condition, and one in good condition. The woman was listed in guarded but stable condition. An all-points bulletin had been issued for her arrest.

- Roxanna Ullery, a 23-year-old bookkeeper at Cinco Construction Company in Orlando, Florida, was acquitted of shooting and killing her boss who had continually sexually harassed her for more than six months. Ullery feared he would rape her. She was convicted of carrying a concealed weapon.

- On September 25, 1987, Eric W. Garcia, 24, upset over an argument with his wife, entered the fireworks factory where he worked, and set off an explosion that injured at least four people, knocked out power to hundreds of homes and sent shock waves felt 30 miles away. Garcia, described by co-workers as a "nice young man," was killed in the blast. Investigators believe that Garcia set off the explosion following a heated argument with his wife the night before. His wife, who also worked for the fireworks factory, called the police just hours before the explosion saying she and her husband were having marital problems and that she feared for his safety and mental welfare.

- On December 14, 1992, as an office Christmas party was breaking up, Alford, an employee of the company, began arguing with his former "live-in" girlfriend. When two co-workers tried to intervene, Alford pulled a gun and shot and killed the girlfriend and both co-workers before hanging himself. Another co-worker was critically wounded and the wife of yet another co-worker was sexually assaulted. The first shots were fired at about 6:30 p.m.

Alford's mother died one week before and he and his live-in girlfriend had recently broken up. About one dozen people were present when the shooting started. One fled to a near-by office and called police. The caller told authorities that Alford was depressed over his mother's death.

Police arrived with crisis negotiators who talked to the gunman for about two hours before officers fired tear gas to force him out of the building. Officers stormed the office, in a warehouse district, about 10:30 p.m. and found the gunman had hanged himself. Alford had been arrested for cocaine possession in 1985 and on burglary and drug charges in 1987.

- In one of the few instances of murder-for-hire, Constantine "Tony" Baruso, a 62-year-old union President, was accused of arranging the June 1, 1981, fatal shootings of two union activists in Seattle, Washington. If convicted, Baruso could face either the death penalty or life imprisonment without parole. The handgun used in the shootings was Baruso's. He claimed it had been stolen. Initially, three Filipino gang (Tulisian) members were charged and convicted of the murders. Prosecutors indicated that there was insufficient evidence to charge Baruso at that point-in-time.

  A later civil lawsuit contended that the slayings were ordered from Manila because of the victims' activism against President Ferdinand Marcos' martial-law regime in the Philippines. Judgments for civil liability were made against Baruso, the Marcos' estate, Marcos' widow, Imelda, and Marcos' friend Dr. Malabed of San Francisco. Evidence in the civil trial indicated that Baruso flew to San Francisco two weeks before the murders, picked up $15,000 from Malabed (who was accused of maintaining a Philippines intelligence "slush fund") keeping $10,000 for himself, and giving $5,000 to the triggermen. Due to the evidence uncovered in the civil trial the indictment was sought. Baruso pled not guilty and was held in jail on $500,000 bail.

- Michael Burns, 37, had worked at the Prescolite factory in Eldorado, Arkansas, for 16 years. On February 3, 1993, he returned from his lunch break through a back entrance of the plant with a gun in each hand and shot eight co-workers, killing one of them, before a wounded man hit Burns in the head with a pipe. Sheriff's officials said Burns was upset because he had been harassed by other workers. A note was found on Burns indicating "he was angry at fellow employees." A co-worker said he had talked to Burns earlier that day and thought he appeared normal. "He didn't act like nobody was messing with him this morning. He was just a guy who come to work every day. He didn't talk much. He acted like he never would do no harm to nobody."

Victims included a 52-year-old male who was killed, 56-year-old and 39-year-old males who were injured, and five others who were injured.

The status of Burns was unknown; however, he was in critical condition after undergoing surgery for a head injury.

- On May 29, 1985, James Darryl Smith, Donnie Thornsbury, David Russell Thornsbury, and Arnold Ray Heightland, all members of United Mine Workers, participated in the slaying of a non-union coal truck driver and the injury of a non-union driver who was helping deliver coal in Pike County, Kentucky. The shooting occurred in an ambush during a 1985 coal workers' strike. The four men were convicted of murder with prison sentences ranging from 30 to 45 years. The federal appeals court upheld the convictions and sentences. All were in federal custody.

Former Employees

- Larry Thomas Hansel was a 41-year-old computer technician, laid off for three months from the Elgar Corporation in San Diego, California. On June 5, 1991, he went looking for three former bosses. He blasted his way into the building where he had worked with a shotgun and rifle. Hansel ended up killing one of his targeted victims, but the other two men escaped. One victim just happened to be in the wrong place at the wrong time. The two victims were found side-by-side in a cubicle on the top floor of the two-story building.

- On February 16, 1988, Richard Farley, 39, a former software engineer at ESL Inc., gained access to the plant by blasting his way through a computer-controlled door. He carried several firearms and opened fire, killing eight people (5 men and 3 women) and wounding three others (2 men and 1 woman), including a former co-worker who had spurned his romantic advances. Two men and one woman were also shot at but uninjured. Farley expended at least 100 rounds during the incident.

  Farley had been fired in 1986 for harassing a female worker. The shooting incident was prompted by a romantic obsession with this former co-worker. At his trial, Farley testified that he planned to kill himself in front of his former co-worker to make her feel guilty for rejecting him for three years and that he "instinctively" shot people who got in his way. The co-worker was shot but survived and testified against him. Farley told police that he wanted her to survive the attack so that she would live to regret her rejection of him. He also said that he would have left her alone if she had gone out with him "just once." Farley had been served with a court order to stay away from her one week before the shotgun slayings. The woman said that fear of the consequences of his written threats caused her to endure the behavior. She had obtained an unlisted phone number and moved three times, until she realized the month before the incident that she was "at the end of her rope." It was then that she obtained the restraining order.

  The prosecutor said Farley had planned the attack and prepared for it by taking target practice and arming himself with more than 1,000 rounds of ammunition. The siege lasted five hours, during which time police hostage negotiators taped one telephone conversation with Farley in which he said, "I hope she'll never do this to anybody else again. She can't play with people's lives." He blamed her for getting him fired by showing company officials a series of letters he had written to her. He also indicated that he only knew one of the 10 people he had shot. He said, "I came down here to do as much damage to equipment at ESL as possible." Farley said on a tape played in court that he quit his shooting spree after "it wasn't fun anymore." He was charged with seven counts of murder and five counts of attempted murder, as well as charges of burglary, vandalism, and assault with a deadly weapon.

Farley had no criminal record, had been honorably discharged from the Navy, was highly intelligent, and performed satisfactorily at several top-secret defense jobs. He was a part-time computer science student at a local university and was engaged to marry another computer science student. He was known as "competent, cheerful, a pretty nice guy," according to his employer.

- Stanley Walton, 32, after being fired the day before, returned to the printing company where he had worked for several years and shot two former co-workers with a shotgun, critically wounding them. He was arrested at the plant shortly after the shootings and charged with four counts of aggravated assault. The victims were both men, ages 49 and 52. Walton had been fired for violating company rules.

Customer Violence in Service Organizations

- On October 14, 1993, during the noontime rush, James M. Buquet, 19, drove up to the Family Fitness Center in El Cajon, California, where he was a member. He shot and killed a man who was leaving the club, walked into the club and killed two female instructors and a female customer with a shotgun, before he proceeded to his car and killed himself.

    The three women died at the scene. The man died shortly afterward at the hospital. Another woman suffered minor injuries. One instructor indicated that a few hundred people, including 5-10 children in the baby-sitting area, were in the building when Buquet entered.

    The specific motive for this incident was unknown; however, the incident involved Buquet's ex-wife, who was a member of the club. The victims included a female customer, 19, who was killed while standing in the lobby; a 36-year-old female instructor who died; a 37-year-old man who was killed while leaving the health club; and an injured female, age unknown.

- This customer expressed his dissatisfaction immediately and with lethal violence. Michael Vernon, 22, had some history with the shoe store. He had been going there every Tuesday for some time. Each time, the store failed to have his size in the specific pair of sneakers he wanted. This Tuesday, December 19, 1995, Vernon was prepared. When his size shoe wasn't available, he took out a 9mm handgun and began firing. The victims were the 41-year-old wife of the owner, a 12-year-old boy, and two men in their 20s. The owner of the store witnessed the shooting through a peephole in a back room of the store. One woman managed to slip outside as the gunfire began and flagged down a highway patrol officer.

The officer took cover behind a car parked in front of the store. When Vernon fled the store, holding a hostage, the officer fired at least four shots with his shotgun and wounded Vernon. The wounded suspect continued to flee and was spotted by two transit cops who were eating lunch in a restaurant located on the same block as the shoe store. The transit officers chased Vernon around the corner where he was confronted by an off-duty cop assigned to the Bronx Task Force. Vernon collapsed and was arrested. Three men were critically injured in the shootout between Vernon and the police.

Vernon, who lived in a drug- and gun-infested project, was known to come from a large, troubled family. He lived with his mother. His father had died several years before, his brother died two years before from AIDS contracted after exposure to an infected needle. Vernon had a history of violence. He had fired shots at a cab driver during the summer over a fare dispute. He had been institutionalized briefly a couple of months earlier for mental illness. One neighbor said he was "the devil's child" (Cheng & Polner, 1995).

- One of the multiple-site incidents occurred Saturday, November 7, 1992, when Lynwood "Crazy Jim" Drake II, a 43-year-old unemployed construction worker, killed six people and wounded another at three different locations before killing himself. He had planned to kill his pastor and a day-care worker who had cared for his child but was prohibited by car trouble. Drake wanted to avenge his gambling losses and his eviction for nonpayment of rent. He considered these people his enemies.

  Drake left a suicide note identifying himself as Jesse Cole Younger. In the note he harshly criticized his parents and a sister for his troubles, saying he had faced lifelong persecution.

"They refused to help. Damn the American family to hell. God forgive me."

The "shooting rampage" started in Morro Bay, California, a seaside resort of 10,000 about 220 miles north of Los Angeles, where he was known as "Crazy Jim." He "hunted down" his former landlord and fatally shot him in the throat with a hand-gun while the man was preparing dinner. He then went to a second house and killed two men and wounded another who had helped the landlord to evict him. Drake next went 40 miles to a card room in Paso Robles where he fatally shot two dealers and a customer with a shotgun. He had lost several hundred dollars at the card tables, been unsuccessful in obtaining credit, and was angry at the victims for telling him to stop cheating. Authorities tracked him to a nearby town to the home of a woman from whom he had once rented. Authorities used the telephone to try to get him to surrender. He shot himself to death there early Sunday.

Apparently he had told many people that he would some-day kill his enemies and himself, but he was considered such a "nut" that nobody took him seriously. Authorities said the most recent threat came on the day of the incident, but nobody called the police. A sheriff's Sergeant said, "Nobody, I mean nobody, called anybody about that [the threat that day]. They knew this guy. This guy is a nut. All of them used the word nut. That's not my word. And they didn't believe him." At scene 1, the victim killed was the 80-year-old, male, former landlord; at scene 2, two men who had helped the former landlord with the eviction were killed, and one other man was wounded; and at scene 3, two card dealers and a customer were killed after they told Drake to stop cheating.

- On Tuesday, February 23, 1990, Clifford J. Harper, 39, sat in an all-night restaurant for three hours before drawing a pistol, shooting an employee to death, and critically wounding a cus-tomer. He was shot by police as he left the restaurant. Harp-er had been staying in a motel in this secluded college town of 35,000 in western Montana.

  Killed was a 64-year-old male employee while a 40-year-old male customer was critically injured. The motive for this incident was unknown.

- A man who was frustrated because he could not withdraw $98,000 in cash from his bank account sought retaliation when he splashed sulfuric acid on the police who tried to arrest him. Eleven people were injured in the incident. Seventy-year-old Anthony Caggiano had apparently come to the bank in the early morning attempting to withdraw the money, at which time he was told that the amount was too large to provide in cash, but that he could have the money in checks. He later returned with a wrench and sulfuric acid. Caggiano began smashing the windows with the wrench and splashed acid on anyone who came near him. He was later charged with assault, criminal mischief, resisting arrest, menacing, and criminal possession of a dangerous weapon.

- On June 9, 1986, Lawrence Timmons, 41, of Forth Worth, Texas, was shot about 3:30 a.m. after a fight touched off by the lack of large buns at a 24-hour hamburger stand. Timmons was shot by a county sheriff, who was moonlighting as a security guard. After Timmons had become loud and abusive when he discovered the restaurant had run out of large buns, the security guard/sheriff took Timmons outside to arrest him. As he did so, Timmons pulled a knife on the officer, took his nightstick, and began beating him with it. The officer was able to draw his gun and shoot Timmons, who was pronounced dead at the hospital.

Customer Violence in Government/Institutions

- On October 24, 1990, a juvenile stabbed his physics teacher after a dispute over a test grade. The juvenile had no history of violence and was a straight "A" student. The juvenile was charged with attempted murder.

- Shortly after 9:00 a.m. on May 3, 1988, Kurt M. Allen entered the post office in search of his Social Security check. When the check could not be found he appeared angry and confronted the male clerk who was staffing the general delivery window. Allen became more and more angry. The clerk tried to calm him. Allen pulled a gun and shot at the clerk who ducked and received a scalp wound which was treated at the scene. A male postal security officer confronted Allen, who fired several shots with a handgun, wounding the officer in the upper arm. The officer returned fire, wounding Allen in the buttocks. Allen was arrested by police officers outside the post office.

- On February 23, 1988, a disgruntled workers' compensation recipient pulled a .38 caliber handgun in the Workers Compensation Board hearing room and held two attorneys hostage. He released them before surrendering to police. No one was injured in the incident. One of the attorneys had represented the individual in the workers' compensation trial. The other attorney was an administrative law judge.

    The gunman's only demand was to meet with John Johnson, a local television news reporter, who came to the scene and allowed the gunman to air his grievances about the case. The gunman complained to Johnson that he was being harassed over the $20,000 settlement in his case. Workers' Compensation Board Chairman, Barbara Patton, agreed to review the case, which involved a 1984 car accident that led to a settlement in December 1987.

Customer Violence in Manufacturing Organizations

No cases are presented because this category was not reflected in the data. This finding was expected because these types of organizations do not have the type of face-to-face customer base that is experienced in service and government organizations.

Domestic-Related Violence in Service Organizations

- On Saturday, September 12, 1992, after the Epcot Center at Disney World, Florida, had closed, Allen J. Ferris demanded to see his ex-girlfriend, a Disney World employee. Ferris, 37, was distressed over the breakup of an eight-year relationship.

When his demands were refused, he pulled a 12-gauge shotgun from a tote bag and fired three times at the first guard, who fled unharmed. The other two guards also ran but they stopped when Ferris fired again and they were taken hostage in a restroom for about 10 minutes. When Sheriff's deputies surrounded the area, Ferris released the hostages and begged the sheriff deputies to kill him. Ferris then proceeded to take his own life.

- A 37-year-old gunman armed with a .357 magnum, who had a history of alcohol and drug abuse, held five people hostage in a downtown Indianapolis office building for 16 hours. Before Richard Beatty released the last hostage, his former girlfriend, he requested that his attorney draw up a will for him and that he be allowed to scatter $500,000 in cash over the city. He also demanded that his former girlfriend not lose her job over the incident. During the course of events, he was allegedly taking drugs to stay awake. After the incident, Beatty's mother indicated that she "was glad he didn't get stupid," and kill himself.

- On August 2, 1982, George Wallace, 40, entered a bar in Pasadena, Texas, and opened fire, wounding his ex-girlfriend and killing her daughter. When stopped by police while fleeing the scene, Wallace shot himself. He used a .38 caliber revolver he bought at a pawn shop hours earlier.

- One of the most unusual forms of lethal domestic violence in the workplace also had unintended consequences. Lewis Allen Harry, Jr., 32, of Phoenix, Arizona, was arrested on four counts of attempted murder and later charged with one count of first-degree murder. He was accused of placing sodium cyanide, a deadly poison, in the bottled water at an insurance office where a 46-year-old woman died after drinking from the water cooler on Monday, March 24, 1986. Harry's wife worked with the victim in the insurance office. He worked in the physical education department as an equipment manager at South Mountain Community College in Phoenix.

   This poisoning incident was Harry's second alleged attempt to kill his wife. One of the attempted murder charges accused him of putting poison in his wife's scotch bottle on March 21. The other attempted murder counts involved two office workers who drank from the poisoned bottled water, but spit it out because of the taste. They suffered no ill effects. An autopsy showed that the employee died of cyanide poisoning and classified the death as homicide. Harry is believed to have poisoned the water sometime over the weekend.

- A reputed gang member, Humberto De La Torre, 21, was sentenced to 625 years to life in prison for the September 1982 torching of a residential hotel where his family lived. De La Torre admitted setting the hotel fire that killed 25 people, including six members of his own family. He will not be eligible for parole for 312 years under what may be the longest prison sentence ever given in the State of California. One of the survivors of the blaze asked the judge to give the defendant the death penalty because of the three daughters, one son, seven grandchildren, one daughter-in-law and one son-in-law he lost in the blaze. De La Torre was ineligible for the death penalty because it was not sought by the prosecution. Police said that De La Torre confessed setting the fire to get revenge on his uncle, the manager of the hotel, because the man had warned him to stay away from the building because he was a reputed gang member. In exchange for his guilty plea to one count of first-degree murder for each of the 13 children, 11 adults, and one fetus who died in the blaze, the judge dismissed a burglary and arson charge and special circumstances that could have qualified him for the death penalty or a prison term of life without the possibility of parole.

- February 24, 1984, in Merlin, Oregon, a man identified as John Carter burst into a pizza parlor before it opened for business and told a male employee to "Get the hell out of here." The employee ran from the pizza parlor to a grocery store next door and used the telephone to contact police. Carter held his former wife and her boss at gunpoint in the pizza parlor where his ex-wife worked. They were held for as long as five hours before Carter opened fire. The hostages were killed in separate rooms by gunshots to the face and head. Carter then turned the gun on himself and was critically wounded by a bullet wound to the forehead.

Due to the construction of the building, police who surrounded it did not hear the gunshots that killed the victims. They were able to hear the shot that wounded Carter, and they entered the building and found him wounded, and the two dead bodies. Sheriff deputies said the hostages could have been dead for several hours before the gunman shot himself. Oregon State Police troopers and sheriff's deputies had negotiated with the gunman for five hours by telephone from the grocery store next door before the incident ended.

- It was Friday, October 21, 1995. A customer was talking with a loan officer at the National City Bank in Carmel, Indiana. A man walked calmly into the office, ordered the customer to leave, closed the door to the office and fired two shots which, police later learned, killed both of them. The loan officer, Donna J. Montgomery, had filed a divorce petition on Tuesday from her husband, Robert J. Montgomery, a self-employed farmer and automobile broker. A restraining order was also issued against Mr. Montgomery saying that the couple had been separated and that Mrs. Montgomery was seeking the divorce because of her husband's violent and threatening behavior.

  Police surrounded the two story building and helped 27 people escape through windows. Some bank employees hid in the vault before escaping. This strategy was used by those seeking protection in a number of other cases where a vault was available. One of the bank customers said that all the women started screaming and running. When four more pops were heard, this customer jumped up, tripped over something, and ran out the front door.

  Not knowing that the man had killed himself, police tried to contact him by telephone but got no response. At one point, police asked the local television station to stop showing live pictures of officers from the scene in order to shield their movements from what they believed to be a barricaded suspect situation. The bodies of Mr. and Mrs. Montgomery were found five hours later when the police entered Mrs. Montgomery's office (Wyman, 1995).

- The date was Wednesday, August 17, 1988. The location was a crowded Atlanta, Georgia, hospital emergency room. James Howard, Jr., 51, drew a gun from under his brown security guard uniform shirt and opened fire. Howard fired five shots at his wife, 36 and her male companion, 29, then put the gun to his head and killed himself with the sixth bullet. His estranged wife was wounded so gravely that she died the next day; the man who had accompanied her to the emergency room was also killed. Two other people received minor injuries from bullet fragments and were treated and released.

  Howard had entered the emergency room about 6:30 p.m. where he found his wife awaiting treatment for a leg injury. He engaged in a "quiet but intense" argument with her but nobody seemed to know what the argument was about. The relationship between Mrs. Howard and her companion was unknown and police detectives had no explanation for the shooting.

  Witnesses reported hearing shots and someone screaming for everyone to "Get out! Get down!" while everyone was running and screaming. "It was crazy, panic, people running everywhere." Some reported ducking into rooms off the side of the emergency room to escape.

Domestic-Related Violence in Government/Institutions

- Mrs. Nora V. Broomall, 52, was found guilty of paying Cecil E. Booher, 36, $25,000 to kill her husband on October 9, 1987, in hopes of collecting a $100,000 insurance policy. Both Broomall and Booher were given life sentences on the murder charges. The victim, George Broomall, 50, was stabbed twice in the chest and his throat was slashed. He was found in an upstairs hallway at the Callanwolde Fine Arts Center in Decatur, Georgia, where he had been a maintenance worker.

- On Sunday morning, September 19, 1993, Elizabeth Mayberry shot to death Reverend Roland Phillips as he was finishing a sermon in the United Methodist Church where he was part-time pastor in New Salem, Indiana. Mayberry was upset after being rejected by Phillips. According to a witness she said, "If I can't have you, ain't nobody can have you." The 78-year-old witness helped wrestle Mayberry to the floor and held her until police arrived. None of the 25 people in the congregation, including Phillips' 13-year-old daughter were injured.

Mayberry and Phillips met in April 1992 when he spoke at a conference for singles. They dated for four months and he broke up with her in August 1992. Mayberry lost weight and became withdrawn after the breakup. Her minister indicated that she had been troubled and depressed. Mayberry, a 36-year-old artist for the local newspaper, was arrested, charged with murder, and held without bond. She could face the death penalty if convicted of murder.

- A 21-year-old clerk typist died instantly after being shot by her 23-year-old husband near her office in the Department of Labor. Police sources indicated that they did not know if the couple had had arguments in the past. The couple did, however, argue prior to the offender shooting his wife with a .38 caliber revolver twice in the head. There were several witnesses to the incident, none of whom were injured. Although several thousand employees work in the building, routine security checks are not done during the day, thus enabling the offender to enter the building with a gun without difficulty.

- On December 9, 1989, Larry Bates, 35, angered that his wife had filed for divorce, threatened he would return to a Natchez, Mississippi, primary school with a gun. His wife, a 40-year-old teacher's aide did not inform anyone of this threat. Approximately 1½ hours later he returned to her classroom armed with a .38 caliber pistol and proclaimed that the kindergarten classroom was "under siege." When the police finally were able to arrest Bates, he had raped two other teachers and shot his wife twice, once in the back and once in the head. Although none of the children were physically injured, he used them as shields by having them line up against the windows so that police could not shoot into the classroom.

- The only non-intimate domestic-related violence occurred on the morning of November 1, 1993, when John Albro, approximately 30 years old, opened fire in the town office building, killing two female employees and critically wounding a third, the town's administrative assistant, before shooting himself. Albro was seriously injured. He is the son of one of the town's three selectmen (a part-time position). His father was not in the building at the time. Mr. Albro was a troubled individual who had a history of complaints and troubled behavior. Gun shells were strewn about in the section that contains the selectmen's office. Newbury, New Hampshire, is a resort community on Lake Sunapee, about 30 miles northwest of Concord (population 1,350).

Domestic-Related Violence in Manufacturing Organizations

Only two incidents of this type occurred in our study. One is presented here. To be considered in this category, the domestic violence must be committed by someone other than an employee who has an intimate or familial relationship with an individual employed by the organization.

- One day after a 25-year-old receptionist had warned security guards to watch for her former boyfriend and make sure that he did not get on the grounds, Edward Fountain, Jr., 28, scaled the fence, proceeded directly to her post, and fatally shot her twice in the chest. Two supervisors were injured while trying to intervene. The woman had worked at the plant for two years. She and Fountain had recently argued and that argument was thought to have prompted the shooting.

    Fountain had illegally entered the grounds of the company on a previous occasion. The site consists of 500 acres, enclosed within a six-foot high fence that is topped with three strands of barbed wire.

    Fountain was arrested without incident at the scene following the shootings. He was charged with first-degree murder, first-degree attempted murder, assault, and a weapons violation.

The injured were a 46-year-old male control supervisor and a 56-year-old male associate director of the company. Both of these men were in the first-floor reception area when the gunman entered and the confrontation unfolded. They were treated at a local hospital and released.

PRACTICE EXERCISE FOR CHAPTER 3

The intent of the practice exercises is to encourage the reader to use critical thinking skills in planning for and possibly preventing incidents of workplace violence. Often there are no right or wrong answers because each situation is different depending on the workplace setting and the individuals involved. The reader has different levels of information available as he/she proceeds through the text; however, each exercise should be attempted given the current information available. After reading the remainder of the text, the reader might choose to come back to earlier exercises and examine the answers to see if he/she would change them in light of added information.

The following exercise focuses on the experiences of a particular employee who has been treated badly by his co-workers. The reader is asked to identify warning indicators of the incident and to determine what actions might have been taken to prevent the incident.

The Incident of the Teased Employee

The following fictitious case is based on a true story in which co-workers so hurt an individual emotionally over time that he became enraged enough to be driven to lethal workplace violence.

Edward Fitzpatrick was a mechanic for a mass-transit rail system in a major metropolitan center of the midwest. He was 28 years old and had been working for FairRail Transit System for five years when he took a 9mm handgun with him to work. As he arrived at his work station, his supervisor and three co-workers were already at their posts to begin this high stress job of maintaining the equipment on which hundreds of thousands of workers commuted each day. Edward had his handgun drawn before entering the small building where they met before going out to work each day. As he came through the door, Fitzpatrick began firing. He saved one shot for himself.

The three co-workers and Fitzpatrick died immediately. Fitzpatrick's supervisor lived to tell the story. He described Fitzpatrick as a quiet, shy young man with a speech impediment. The supervisor said that Fitzpatrick's co-workers often teased him about it and he seemed to take everything in stride. The supervisor could not believe that Fitzpatrick would commit such violence. He appeared to be such a gentle man.

Two neighbors were the only people who seemed to really know Fitzpatrick. Both were saddened by the events. Fitzpatrick had confided to both of them individually about what he considered to be the unmerciful teasing that he was exposed to at work concerning his speech impediment. His co-workers called him names and mocked him. There was nobody to take up for him, not even his supervisor. The supervisor had never taken part in the "good fun" that everyone was having at Fitzpatrick's expense, but Fitzpatrick was hurt that his supervisor didn't make them stop.

Fitzpatrick had no family, just these two friends who only knew him because they were neighbors. He watched out for them and they tried to give him emotional support. Both friends were aware that he was getting increasingly more upset about his mistreatment but neither knew what to do about it. They felt all they could do was wait and pray.

Your Task

1. First, consider this case in specific. List the warning signs that co-workers or Fitzpatrick's supervisor might have overlooked that would have indicated that this individual might commit an act of violence in the workplace.

_____

_____

_____

2. Why do you think nobody in the workplace recognized how hurt Fitzpatrick was by their behavior?

_____

_____

_____

3. What actions do you think should have been taken by co-workers in this incident?

_____

_____

_____

4. If a person in *your* organization were to tease or mock a co-worker:

    a. How would other employees in the organization respond?

    _____

    _____

    _____

    b. How would supervisors respond?

    _____

    _____

    _____

    c. What should co-workers do to effectively respond to this situation?

    _____

    _____

    _____

    d. What should supervisors do to effectively respond to this situation?

    _____

    _____

4

Preventing
Workplace Violence

Introduction

The issue of violence in the workplace has prompted a number of corporations to initiate preventive measures and increased physical security. However, it would be unrealistic to think that workplace violence could be entirely prevented. Certainly, it is within an employer's control to reduce and possibly lessen the impact of workplace violence with proper planning. Unfortunately, better lighting, access control, the number of security officers, or other physical security techniques are not a panacea. There is no empirical data to support that any one of these measures can prevent an occupational violent incident. At some level, after pre-employment screening, counseling, and prevention programs have been implemented, employers must look beyond to the underlying causes of fear, frustration, and anger. Unfortunately, violence is becoming an acceptable method of interpersonal communication.

Violent crimes have traditionally been viewed as a law enforcement and criminal justice problem. What was once considered to occur primarily in the urban cities and alleyways, crimes of violence, murder and aggravated assault, have become crimes of the workplace. When looked at in perspective, this phenomena should not come as a surprise. For example, the second leading cause of death for all 15- to

24-year-old individuals in the United States was homicide. In 1980, acts of violence accounted for 350,000 hospitalizations, 1.5 million hospital days, and 640 million in health care costs (Baker, 1982).

The word prevention, as it's definition implies, suggests that something can be caused not to happen. Although there is generally an agreement among researchers and experts that violent behavior cannot be predicted with any certainty, the Center for Disease Control (CDC) and federal regulators such as the Occupational Safety and Health Administration (OSHA), indicate that many workplace murders are in fact preventable. This position by CDC epidemiologists and federal regulators is supported by a recent Florida Court of Appeals decision that the Circle K Corporation can be held liable for failing to take action that might have prevented the murder of a 27-year-old clerk by a robber. These experts contend that many workplace murders are preventable and, as a consequence, constitute possible violations of the "general duty clause" of the Occupational Safety and Health Act of 1970.

The general duty clause requires employers to provide workers with a safe workplace. Any injury or illness that occurs as a result of workplace violence is to be recorded on the employers OSHA 200 log which is used by all employers to document all workplace injury and illness. This log however is not required for workplaces with fewer than 10 employees, which means that any incident of violence in small businesses is going unrecorded.

Currently, there is a consensus building in the legislature to eliminate the general duty clause, and if this happens, workplace violence may take a back seat with OSHA. At the same time, however, there is pressure on OSHA to take a more active role with regard to WV even to the point of requiring specific physical security guidelines. A NIOSH task force is currently studying convenience store designs to develop safety measures. Some states have even gone so far as to pass laws requiring specific physical security measures. For example the state of Florida passed legislation to require stores to install cameras and have at least two clerks working all shifts. (Solomon & King, 1993).

An April 1995 memorandum from OSHA to all state OSHA designees states that OSHA's goal with regard to workplace violence is to assure that employers are taking measures to adequately protect their employees from this workplace hazard. The memorandum further indicates that they are currently in the process of developing guidelines to educate and communicate to employers how to "prevent" and protect workers from violence on the job. Also, the Department of Labor's Technical Data Center (TDC) maintains and updates a file containing reference materials on violence in the workplace and is currently developing a database which will hopefully make workplace violence information more accessible. Additionally, the office of the Directorate of Compliance Programs is collecting information on each worker complaint either formal or non-formal referral, or fatality/catastrophe report. The information collected includes the following:

1. Type of industry and establishment;

2. What type(s) of violence are the subject of the complaint;

3. Has the worker complained to a supervisor or other manager about the situation?

4. What was the manager's or supervisor's response to the worker?

5. What precautions, if any, were taken by management or employees?

6. Did a violent incident actually occur?

7. Were workers killed or injured? If so what types of injury did they sustain?

8. Were there previous, similar incidents at this workplace?

9. How many employees were involved in or exposed to the incident or the condition complained about?

10. Does the employer have a crisis plan or program that addresses the problem?

11. Are employees trained to implement the plan or program?

12. What feasible means of abatement are available to resolve the condition?

Currently OSHA is accepting all complaints and referrals on workplace violence. As of this writing however, OSHA's position is that before a general duty citation is issued it must meet the following criteria: (1) complete development of case file documentation, (2) early involvement of OSHA's Regional Solicitor in the investigation of the case, (3) concurrence of the Director of Compliance programs, and (4) expert witnesses are also required in the development and litigation of any citations. If the complaint does not meet the above criteria, then OSHA issues only an advisory letter and not a general duty clause citation. Most compelling, only one workplace violence citation was isuued out of 1,000 general duty clause citations from June 1994 to June 1995. In this one incident on the night of April 21, 1994, two separate Dairy Barn stores were robbed by the same group of perpetrators. Dairy Barn is a chain of 60 company owned and operated drive-thru convenience stores on Long Island. There was a single male employee age 45 at one of the Dairy Barns who was shot with a firearm and killed. The two employees at the other store, both males ages 41 and 18, were shot with a firearm but survived. Consequently, to obtain a more accurate picture of the number of workplace violent incidents reported to OSHA, the "advisory letter," would serve as a more accurate source.

The general guidelines for reporting workplace violence by employers begin with a decision of whether or not it is work related. OSHA determines whether or not something is work-related based upon the following reportable events: if an employee is shot and killed at work by a fellow employee, if an employee in a convenience store is killed during an attempted robbery, if an employee is killed in a commercial airliner crash while returning home from a business trip, and if an employee is killed in an automobile crash while driving to or from a train station on a business trip.

Once the case is deemed to be work-related, its recordability depends on whether it is an injury that involves loss of consciousness, job transfer, restriction of work or motion, medical treatment beyond first aid, or is an occupational illness. Moreover, all work-related fatalities are recordable and reportable and work-related cases involving days away from work and/or days of restricted work activity are recordable. The reporting guideline for workplace fatalities is within the first eight hours, and if there are three or more people requiring hospitalization, a report must be filed under OSHA 29 CFR 1904.8, including those resulting from workplace violence.

Workplace Violence Prevention Techniques

An investigation into workplace violence is most likely to occur when an area OSHA director has received complaints of serious alleged violations and the employer has not taken any action to correct the problem. Presently, OSHA is only issuing what is referred to as "5(a)(1)," letters that define the hazards employees are exposed to and the abatement methods to be implemented. At the time of this research there were only a few states that had developed specific abatement guidelines to "prevent" workplace violence. California has developed by far some of the most comprehensive workplace violence guidelines. These guidelines were based upon a broad public advisory process initiated at a Conference on Workplace Security held in Los Angeles in April of 1994 and continued at a Second conference held in San Francisco in November of 1994. (See page 99, this text.)

The CAL/OSHA study bases much of their prevention guidelines on what they have identified as three types of workplace violence events that can occur. In Type I, the perpetrator has no legitimate business relationship to the workplace and usually enters the affected workplace to commit a robbery or other criminal act. The Type II perpetrator is either the recipient, or the object, of a service provided by the affected workplace or the victim, e.g., the assailant, is a current or former client, patient, customer, passenger, criminal suspect, inmate or prisoner. Finally in Type III, the agent has some employment-related involvement with the workplace. Usually this involves an assault by a current or former employee, supervisor or manager, by a current/former spouse or lover, a relative or friend, or some other person who has a dispute with an employee of the affected workplace. The research presented in Chapter 2 and the incidents presented in Chapter 3 focused on Type II and Type III incidents.

According to CAL/OSHA the characteristics of the establishments affected, the profile and motive of the perpetrator or assailant, and the preventive measures differ for each of the three major types of workplace violence events. The guidelines describe the characteristics of each of the different types of events as follows:

CHARACTERISTICS OF TYPE I EVENTS

In California, the majority (60%) of workplace homicides involve a person entering a small late-night retail establishment, e.g., liquor store, gas station or a convenience food store, to commit a robbery. During the commission of the robbery, an employee or, more likely, the proprietor is killed or injured.

Employees or proprietors who have face-to-face contact and exchange money with the public, work late at night and into the early morning hours, and work alone or in very small numbers are at greatest risk of a Type I event. While the assailant may feign being a customer as a pretext to enter the establishment, he or she has no legitimate business relationship to the workplace.

Retail robberies resulting in workplace assaults usually occur between the hours of eleven in the evening and six in the morning and are most often armed (gun or knife) robberies. In addition to employees who are classified as cashiers, many victims of late night retail violence are supervisors or proprietors who are attacked while locking up their establishment for the night and janitors who are assaulted while cleaning the establishment after it is closed.

Other occupations/workplaces may be at risk of a Type I event. For instance, assaults on taxicab drivers also involve a pattern similar to retail robberies. The attack is likely to involve an assailant pretending to be a bona fide passenger during the late night or early morning hours who enters the taxicab to rob the driver of his or her fare receipts. Type I events also involve assaults on security guards. It has been known for some time that security guards are at risk of assault when protecting valuable property which is the object of an armed robbery.

CHARACTERISTICS OF TYPE II EVENTS

A Type II workplace violence event involves an assault by someone who is either the recipient or the object of a service provided by the affected workplace or the victim.

Even though Type I events represent the most common type of fatal event in California, fatal Type II events involving victims who provide services to the public are also increasing. In 1993, fatal Type II events accounted for 30% of workplace homicides. Further, when more occupation-specific data about nonfatal workplace violence becomes available, nonfatal Type II events involving assaults to service providers, especially to health care providers, may represent the most prevalent category of workplace violence resulting in physical injury.

Type II events involve fatal or nonfatal injuries to individuals who provide services to the public. These events involve assaults on public safety and correctional personnel, municipal bus or railway drives, health care and social service providers, teachers, sales personnel, and other public or private service sector employees who provide professional, public safety, administrative or business services to the public.

Law enforcement personnel are at risk of assault from the "object" of public safety services (suspicious persons, detainees, or arrestees) when making arrests, conducting drug raids, responding to calls involving robberies or domestic disputes, serving warrants and eviction notices and investigating suspicious vehicles. Similarly, correctional personnel are at risk of assault while guarding or transporting jail or prison inmates.

Of increasing concern, though, are Type II events involving assaults to the following types of service providers:

1. Medical care providers in acute care hospitals, long-term care facilities, outpatient clinics and home health agencies;

2. Mental health and psychiatric care providers at inpatient facilities, outpatient clinics, residential sites and home health agencies;

3. Alcohol and drug treatment providers;

4. Social welfare service providers in unemployment offices, welfare eligibility offices, homeless shelters, probation offices, and child welfare agencies;

5. Teaching, administrative and support staff in schools where students have a history of violent behavior; and

6. Other types of service providers, e.g., justice system personnel, customer service representatives and delivery personnel.

CHARACTERISTICS OF TYPE III EVENTS

A Type III workplace violence event consists of an assault by an individual who has some employment-related involvement with the workplace. Generally, a Type III event involves a threat of violence, or a physical act of violence resulting in a fatal or nonfatal injury, to an employee, supervisor, or manager of the affected workplace by the following types of individuals:

1. A current or former employee, supervisor or manager; or

2. Some other person who has a dispute with an employee of the affected workplace, e.g., current/former spouse or lover, relative, friend or acquaintance.

Type III events account for a much smaller proportion of fatal workplace injuries in California than do Types I and II. For instance, in 1993, Type III events accounted for only 10% of workplace homicides. Nevertheless, Type III fatalities often attract significant media attention and are incorrectly characterized by many as representing "the" workplace violence problem. In fact, it is their media visibility which makes them appear much more common than they actually are.

Most commonly, the primary target of a Type III event is a co-employee, a supervisor or manager of the assailant. In committing a Type III assault, an individual may be seeking revenge for what he or she perceives as unfair treatment by a co-employee, a supervisor or a manager. Increasingly, Type III events involve domestic or romantic disputes in which an employee is threatened in their workplace by an individual with whom they have a personal relationship outside of work.

Given these different types of events and accompanying characteristics, the CAL/OSHA guideline for workplace prevention strategies makes the following recommendations:

I. Initial Assessment

If one or more of the following factors is/are present in the workplace, employers should consider their workplace to be at potential risk of violence:

1. Exchange of money;

2. Working alone at night and during early morning hours;

3. Availability of valued items, e.g., money and jewelry;

4. Guarding money or valuable property or possessions;

5. Performing public safety functions in the community;

6. Working with patients, clients, passengers, customers or students known or suspected to have a history of violence, or;

7. Employees with a history of assaults or who have exhibited belligerent, intimidating or threatening behavior to others.

II. Prevention Strategies for Type I Events

Employers with employees who are known to be at risk for Type I events are required to address workplace security hazards to satisfy the regulatory requirement of establishing, implementing and maintaining an effective Injury and Illness Prevention (IIP) Program. (Title 8, California Code of Regulations (CCR), 3203.)

Employers at risk for Type I, II, and III events must include as a part of their establishment's IIP Program:

1. A system for ensuring that employees comply with safe and healthy work practices, including ensuring that all employees, including supervisors and managers, comply with work practices designed to make the workplace more secure and do not engage in threats or physical actions which create a security hazard to other employees, supervisors or managers in the workplace (3203(a)(3)).

2. A system for communicating with employees about workplace security hazards, including a means that employees can use to inform the employer of security hazards at the worksite without fear of reprisal (3203(a)(3)).

3. Procedures for identifying workplace security hazards including scheduled periodic inspections to identify unsafe conditions and work practices whenever the employer is made aware of a new or a previously unrecognized hazard (3203(a)(4)(c)).

4. Procedures for investigating occupational injury or illness arising from a workplace assault or threat of assault (3203(a)(5)).

5. Procedures for correcting unsafe conditions, work practices and work procedures, including workplace security hazards, and with attention to procedures for protecting employees from physical retaliation for reporting threats (3203(a)(6)).

6. Training and instruction about how to recognize workplace security hazards, measures to prevent workplace assaults and what to do when an assault occurs, including emergency action and post-emergency procedures (3203(a)(7)).

Interestingly, in California, OSHA has specifically targeted hospitals, requiring them to conduct a security and safety assessment, to develop a security plan with measures to protect personnel, patients, and visitors from aggressive or violent behavior, track incidents of aggressive or violent behavior, and provide to employees regularly assigned to the emergency department security education and training on a continuing basis (California Health and Safety Code 1257.7 and 1257.8.).

California has also developed a *Model Injury and Illness Prevention Program for Workplace Security,* for employers with a risk for Type I events and a checklist for employers with employees who are known to be at risk of late night retail workplace violence. (See Appendix 4a).

III. Prevention Strategies for Type II Events

1. Training should be provided to all employees on how to effectively defuse hostile situations involving their clients, patients, customers, passengers and members of the general public to whom they must provide services.

2. Access control should be implemented at all entry points to the facility. In certain situations, it is recommended that alarm systems or "panic buttons" be provided as a back-up measure.

3. Another recommendation is the development of a "Buddy" system to be used in specified emergency situations, as well as the presence of security personnel where appropriate.

D. Prevention Strategies for Type III Events

1. It is the responsibility of the employer to maintain accurate information regarding past incidents of assaults, violence or otherwise inappropriate behavior in the workplace.

2. Procedures should be in place to deal with incidents of violence or aggression. Employers are required to develop specific procedures to respond to workplace security hazards and provide training as necessary to their employees, supervisor and managers.

3. "Trigger Incidents" for violence should be handled with care such as layoffs, reduction-in-force, disciplinary actions such as terminations, suspensions, etc.

4. Employers must implement a clear anti-violence management policy, apply the policy consistently and fairly to all employees, including supervisors and managers, and provide appropriate supervisory and employee training in workplace violence prevention.

5. Employers are cautioned about the ever increasing problem of domestic violence spilling over into the workplace. It is incumbent upon the employer to pro-

vide the threatened employee adequate protection, even to the point of having the authority to seek a temporary restraining order/injunction on behalf of an employee when he or she has suffered unlawful violence or a credible threat of violence reasonably likely to be carried out in the workplace.

The guidelines set forth by California OSHA (CAL/OSHA) are some of the most comprehensive in the country. There are also several other states and agencies that have developed similar standards or recommendations such as the Joint Commission on Accreditation of Health Care Organizations', "1995 Accreditation Manuals for Hospitals;" the Metropolitan Chicago Healthcare Council's, "Guidelines for Dealing with Violent or Aggressive Behavior in Public Sector Health Care Facilities;" and the State of Washington Department of Labor and Industries', "Violence in Washington Workplaces, and Study of Assaults on Staff in Washington State Psychiatric Hospitals."

What will be interesting is a future assessment of the effectiveness of these prevention strategies, along with those outlined in OSHA's 1996 "Guidelines for Preventing Workplace Violence for Health Care and Social Service Workers" (OSHA, 1996).

Most of the guidelines written to date focus upon physical security measures. In addition to California, states such as Florida and Indiana have developed minimum guidelines for employers to follow when designing for and application of various physical security systems.

OSHA has set forth very specific "engineering controls and workplace adaptation" measures. Engineering controls, similar to the concept "crime prevention through environmental design (CPTED)," are design techniques that remove or create a barrier between the worker and the hazard. For example, in a health care setting OSHA recommends the following physical security measures by employers:

- Assess any plans for new construction or physical changes to the facility or workplace to eliminate or reduce security hazards.

- Install and regularly maintain alarm systems and other security devices, panic buttons, hand-held alarms or noise devices, cellular phones, and private channel radios where risk is apparent or may be anticipated, and arrange for a reliable response system when an alarm is triggered.

- Provide metal detectors—installed or handheld, where appropriate-to identify guns, knives, or other weapons.
- Closed-circuit video recording for high-risk areas on a 24-hour basis. Public safety is a greater concern than privacy in these situations.
- Place curved mirrors at hallway intersections or concealed areas.
- Enclose nurses' stations, and install deep service counters or bullet-resistant, shatter-proof glass in reception areas, triage, admitting, or client service rooms.
- Provide employee "safe rooms" for use during emergencies.
- Establish "time-out" or seclusion areas with high ceilings without grids for patients acting out and establish separate rooms for criminal patients.
- Provide client or patient waiting rooms designed to maximize comfort and minimize stress.
- Ensure that counseling or patient care rooms have two exits.
- Limit access to staff counseling rooms and treatment rooms controlled by using locked doors.
- Arrange furniture to prevent entrapment of staff. In interview rooms or crisis treatment areas, furniture should be minimal, lightweight, without sharp corners or edges, and/or affixed to the floor. Limit the number of pictures, vases, ashtrays, or other items that can be used as weapons.
- Provide lockable and secure bathrooms for staff members separate from patient- client, and visitor facilities.
- Lock all unused doors to limit access, in accordance with local fire codes.
- Install bright, effective lighting indoors and outdoors.
- Replace burned-out lights, broken windows, and locks.
- Keep automobiles, if used in the field, well-maintained. Always lock automobiles.

Clearly, OSHA has taken bold steps in setting forth numerous abatement guidelines with regard to workplace violence. The lead they have taken has certainly been instrumental in influencing other agencies to do likewise. For example, in a policy statement from the Office of the Solicitor to the Women's Bureau of the Department of Labor, OSHA outlined its role, risk factors for workplace violence, and examples of acceptable abatement measures. These measures were set forth in the NIOSH "Alert," titled "Preventing Homicide in the Workplace." According to the report there are some generally recognized steps that employers can take to minimize the risks of criminal acts against employees. What is required of an employer will vary depending on the facts, which will be unique to each situation. Options include: security programs and devices (such as bullet proofing, where appropriate, and appropriate locks, lights, alarms, etc.); locked drop-safes; well-lit parking lots, openly visible to the public work area; implementing procedures that are less dangerous (such as for storing and transporting money); training (such as in techniques of conflict resolution, nonviolent response, and procedures for responding to criminal threats); electronic surveillance; working in teams rather than alone, etc. (NIOSH, 1993). The memorandum concludes by saying that based upon their legal opinion an employer could be cited under the general duty clause as a result of hazards presented by the potential for criminal acts against its employees in the workplace.

For example in Indiana, OSHA issued a general duty citation in which a retail employer was given the following abatement measures in response to a workplace violence incident:

1. Effectively train employees in conflict resolution and non-violent response;

2. Install and utilize locked drop-safes;

3. Post signs indicating only small cash amounts are kept in the register;

4. Increase the visibility of the work area to the general public;

5. Provide well-lit parking lots;

6. Isolating workers behind bulletproof barriers (Indiana, 1991, in Thomas, 1992, June).

OSHA has defined these and other physical security techniques as traditional abatement methods. They also emphasize the importance of engineering and administrative controls being implemented to curb the threat of crime-related workplace violence. OSHA indicates that engineering controls are the preferred method of controlling a workplace hazard because, they are usually more effective than administrative controls. Engineering controls for workplace violence include installing metal detectors, changing facility layout to create better escape routes for employees, panic alarms and bulletproof glass for window clerks, mobile phones or communications service for motor vehicle drivers and special delivery messengers. Administrative controls that can help to prevent workplace violence include increasing staffing and banning working alone, as well as training employees to protect themselves.

Profiling Violent Employees

The FBI has put together a Multi-Agency Task Force to study workplace violence. Based upon case analysis's they have identified three types of perpetrators (see Appendix 4b: Recognizing Inappropriate Behavior):

1. Disgruntled Employees

2. Obsessive Individuals

3. Chronic Troublemakers

According to the FBI they are seeing a trend toward increasing incidents of violence in the workplace. They indicate that the Postal Service has experienced 34 homicides as a result of workplace violence over the last 10 years. Although incidents of violence have been prevalent in the workplace for some time, it is this phenomenon of homicide in the workplace that is relatively new. The FBI used police reports as data for their research due to the fact that significant statistics were lacking in this area. They found that there were 750-1000 deaths per year in the workplace as a result of violence occuring in the workplace.

The FBI profile for a potential workplace violence perpetrator is described as a disgruntled employee who exhibits excessive involvement with the job, is a loner, has few friends, and lacks a support system. Additionally, the employee often has an obsession with guns and other weapons, has marital problems, has stress on the job, is frequently laid off, lacks social skills, does not get along well with others, is paranoid, and does not trust supervisors or management (see Appendix 4c: Warning Signs of Potentially Violent Offenders).

Typically, the employee is a white male, 30-50 years old, employed 10-15 years, who feels he has a stake in the company and is empowered because of position and seniority. The FBI has identified it as the "Peter Principle," recognizing that the individual has been somewhat of a problem employee and rather than deal with it early on, supervisors have simply given promotions to move the person from place to place or out of their area. Paranoid workers, use of alcohol and drugs, use/availability of weapons, existence of a victim, poor impulse control or ego dysfunction, alliance and compliance, and subjective uneasiness, are all associated with that of an employee prone to violence.

Regarding victimization, the FBI indicates that women have a high rate of being the victim of violence in the workplace which often stems from domestic violence situations. Although women can remove themselves from the home or place where the violence is taking place, it is not always possible to change jobs so that the would-be assailant is unable to locate her. The assailant then turns to the victim's workplace—not necessarily by choice but out of desperation. In other circumstances, romantic relationships may take place in the work environment and when the relationship ends or goes sour, acts of violence take place at the worksite. Warning signs for these types of potentially violent incidents include hang up calls, excessive phone calls, vandalism to vehicles or residence, threats by mail, and the calling of friends (see Appendix 4d).

The FBI indicates that most homicides in the workplace result from domestic violence or the disgruntled employee who uses a handgun to commit the act of violence, which were also used in 70 percent of the incidents in the current research. Davis (1987) also indicates that handguns, overwhelmingly, were found to be the most commonly used firearm.

The current research identified the days of the week that have the highest-incident rates of workplace violence as Wednesday and Friday. Although the data was limited with regard to time of day, previous research has indicated that the highest risk of workplace violence occurred between the hours of 4 p.m. and midnight for both men and women (Davis, Honchar & Suarez, 1987). According to the CDC, 1990 the highest rates occurred between the months of December and March. This research supports their findings with the highest rates occurring in January and February.

Conclusion

The dilemma facing today's corporations, in what has been called these, "violent-critical times," is to find measures that will assist them in providing a safe and harmonious work environment for their employees. With the increased violence in society, it is not surprising that violence is spilling over into the work environment. The possibility of reducing incidents of workplace violence may be increased by taking proactive measures following a thorough assessment of the organization and its employees. Although there has been no single technique that has proven to be completely successful, it highly probable that managers could develop individual plans suited to their organizations which would reduce risk and ultimately prevent these incidents from occurring (see Appendix 4e: Sources of Workplace Violence Prevention).

PRACTICE EXERCISE FOR CHAPTER 4

The intent of the practice exercises is to encourage the reader to use critical thinking skills in planning for and possibly preventing incidents of workplace violence. Often there are no right or wrong answers because each situation is different depending on the workplace setting and the individuals involved. The reader has different levels of information available as he/she proceeds through the text; however, each exercise should be attempted given the current information available. After reading the remainder of the text, the reader might choose to come back to earlier exercises and examine the answers to see if he/she would change them in light of added information.

The following exercise focuses on the frustrated customer who resorts to a threat of lethal violence. The reader is asked to determine which actions should be taken by each of the key players and what might have been done to prevent the incident.

Preventing Lethal Workplace Violence: Under Armed Threat

It's late Friday morning on a hot summer day in a midwestern city. The Retirement and Benefits Administration office is filled with customers waiting to file for their retirement benefits and with claimants anxious about their overdue checks. Because of a breakdown in the changeover of the agency's central office computer, monthly checks have been delayed more than two weeks.

Customer Service Representatives Sally Mason and Becky Gaynor are working the counter this morning, doing their best to explain the delay to the frustrated claimants. Sally is wearing a fancy corsage on her new dress. This is her last day on the job after 30 years of Federal service. Becky is just a newcomer—she started with the agency less than one month ago and is still being trained.

At 11:45 a.m., Office Manager Jim Beacon stops behind Sally. "Are you ready for your big luncheon?" he whispers to let Sally know that she can leave the counter when she finishes with her current customer.

Sally notices that her next customer will probably be Bill Webber—he's already been waiting more than two hours. Webber frequently shows up with one complaint or another and he's always hard to handle. Sally doesn't know it, but today Webber is even more upset. Because of the delay in getting his check, his savings are almost gone. His wife can't find work. He's desperate and ready to do something drastic to get his money.

The last time he came into the office he actually threatened to hit Sally when she said she couldn't produce his check. She now wonders if she should have reported this incident. At the time she thought Webber was probably just having a bad day.

As Sally, Jim and other office personnel leave for Sally's retirement lunch, Assistant Manager Jeanne Franklin puts a "Closed" sign by Sally's place on the counter. Jeanne then tells Becky she's taking a lunch break in the back office. "I skipped breakfast and I'm starving," Jeanne says. "I'll relieve you in a few minutes."

The office is stifling. Becky wipes her forehead with a tissue and looks over the waiting area. Every seat is occupied and, because it's lunchtime, even more customers are arriving. Each newcomer takes a number from the counter dispenser.

Becky calls the next number, 24. Nothing happens. She calls 24 again in a slightly louder voice. Still no response. She calls 25. A man and a woman leave their seats and walk toward Becky. The woman hesitates, letting the man move ahead. Becky thinks the man looks familiar, but she's not sure. She's startled because his face is quite red and he's glaring at her.

I've got 24, and I've got this too," the man growls at Becky while patting his jacket. "Been waitin' hours in this hellhole," he says, his voice growing louder and more strident. "This is worse'n the army. This is the fifth time I've come lookin' for my check, and you'd better have a check for Bill Webber now or else!"

At that, he pulls out a large handgun and points it right at Becky's face, and shouts, "Don't anybody move or I'll blow this woman away!"

What should Becky do to prevent violence and injury and to discourage Bill Webber from using his gun? To help avoid such a threatening incident for Becky, her co-workers, and for the other customers, what should Jeanne Franklin, Sally Mason, or Jim Beacon have done?

1. When Becky sees the gun pointed at her, what should she do?

2. When Assistant Manager Jeanne Franklin hears the alarm, what should she do?

3. What should Customer Service Representative Sally Mason have done before leaving for lunch?

4. What steps should Office Manager Jim Beacon have taken to prevent this and similar incidents?

Source: *What You Should Know About Coping with Threats and Violence in the Federal Workplace.* [Electronic data file]. (Updated October 1995). Washington, DC: U.S. General Services Administration, Public Building Service.

5 Workplace Violence Policies and Procedures

Many of the guidelines set forth by the various different agencies that have made recommendations concerning workplace violence tend to focus on physical security measures. However, equally important, are the policies and procedures adopted by each organization. Although each organizational environment is somewhat different and every organization will need its own site specific responses, there are certain policies and procedures that have universal application.

Without exception, the issue of violence in the workplace should be addressed in every corporate policy and procedure manual. (See Appendix 5a for a model workplace violence policy). The corporate policy and procedure manual should include a section dedicated to workplace violence. That policy should cover several essential components including pre-employment screening, acts of violence and employee disciplinary procedures, termination procedures, pre- and post-event emergency preparedness plans, employee assistance programs or referral policies if applicable, employee training, and a mechanism for reporting incidents of violent behavior that may be a precursor to a violent episode. There should be a comprehensive written plan for dealing with each of these situations.

Pre-Employment Screening

The first step in taking a proactive approach to reducing incidents of workplace violence begins with the pre-employment screening process. This is a dynamic process that is continually affected by current legislation and public opinion about the right of an employer to delve into the past of a potential employee. For example, with the recent Americans with Disabilities Act (ADA) of 1990, employers are required to confine pre-employment inquires concerning the use of illegal drugs to current or recent use. The ADA describes discrimination as using qualification standards, employment tests, (integrity and other psychological tests) or other selection criteria that screen out or tend to screen out an individual with a disability or a class of individuals with disabilities, unless the standard or the test is shown to be job-related for the position in question and is consistent with business necessity. Honesty and integrity tests are written tests designed to identify individuals applying for work in such jobs who might have a relatively high propensity to steal money or property on the job, or who are likely to engage in behavior such as theft of time, poor work habits, etc.

These tests are normally paper and pencil instruments, administered to job applicants at some stage of the screening and selection process. It is estimated that approximately 10,000 business establishments in the United States use honesty and integrity tests. Important to note is that these tests are designed to measure the potential for *nonviolent crimes*. They do not provide any measurable data with regard to an individual's propensity toward violent behavior.

According to the Equal Employment Opportunity Commission (EEOC), this language means that an employer must only demonstrate that a test is job-related and consistent with business necessity, when a direct link exists between performing poorly on the employment test and the disability. A test that screens out individuals for reasons unrelated to a disability does not violate the ADA. The law as it relates to Title VII of the Civil Rights Act parallels that of ADA. Therefore, to ensure compliance with the ADA, employers should use only those testing instruments that have documented reliability and validity for measuring essential job elements.

Another consideration of ADA is how a test is administered. For example, ADA has a provision that deals with the issue of test administration or reasonable accommodation in the testing process. Under the law, this form of discrimination involves failing to select and administer a test concerning employment in the most effective manner. The purpose is to ensure that, when such a test is administered to a job applicant or an employee who has a disability that impairs sensory, manual, or speaking skills, the test results will accurately reflect the skills, aptitude, and all other factors of the applicant or employee that the test purports to measure. The test results must not reflect the impaired sensory, manual, or speaking skills of such employee or applicant (except where such skills are the factors that the test purports to measure). Companies can comply with the requirements of this section of the law by ensuring that test takers are reasonably accommodated in the testing process. For example, a dyslexic applicant will have difficulty reading, and therefore, should be given an oral, rather than a written, test. However, the law provides that if the test is used to assess reading and if reading is an essential function of the job, such a testing accommodation is unnecessary. To ensure that appropriate arrangements are available, applicants should be made aware that testing will be conducted, and they should be invited to request accommodations prior to the test.

The question of whether or not psychological testing is considered a medical examination under ADA is not clear. The ADA provision states that no medical examination may take place at the pre-offer screening stage but may be conducted only after a conditional offer of employment has been made to the job applicant.

Case law has directed the EEOC in setting forth guidelines regarding psychological testing under ADA. The 1989 landmark case of *Daley v. Koch*, involved the hiring of a police officer. In this case Daley was a candidate for the New York City Police Department and was denied employment based upon the results of two psychological tests, as well as a follow-up interview with the employer's psychologist. Although the applicant was rejected he was not diagnosed as having any specific mental disorder. The Court of Appeals ruled in favor of the employer stating that the traits assessed by the tests do not amount to a mental condition that Congress intended to be considered an impairment that substantially limits a major life activity; therefore, a person having those traits or perceived as having those traits cannot be considered a handicapped person within the meaning of the Act. The prevailing opinion is that to the extent that a test or scales are used to assess personality traits, behavior, attitudes, or propensity to act, when there are not symptoms of a mental disorder, such a test may be used in pre-employment screening. However, test questions regarding mental and physical problems such as whether or not someone received therapy should only be asked after a tentative offer has been extended. An example of a test that asks this type of question would be the Minnesota Multiphasic Personality Inventory (MMPI). If a test of this kind is used by an employer it should be administered only after a job offer is made. As of January of 1994, there have been no legal challenges made regarding the use of pre-employment psychological testing. The majority of complaints have related more to wrongful discharge or reasonable accommodation, rather than hiring practices. However, it is predicted that diagnostic testing will become more of an issue in the future.

A case in point is the growing criticism by the American Postal Workers Union (APWU) against pre-employment screening. Union representatives and postal service employees view pre-employment screening as a "scheme" by the postal service to create a "blame-the-worker" strategy. There are also concerns that pre-employment screening is a potentially dangerous effort to screen out workers that may show tendencies toward violent behavior. Questions regarding a worker's right to privacy have been raised and union representatives argue that so-called indicators of violence cannot be validated as predictive beyond two or three years. As far as the APWU is concerned pre-employment screening, worker profiling and abusive uses of discipline are all blame-the-worker tactics that emphasize the double standard between workers and managers. According to the APWU, these techniques are nothing more than "red herrings" to draw attention away from the long-standing managerial problems confronting the Postal Service.

The irony of all this is that courts are holding employers liable for negligent hiring practices if the employer does not adequately screen potential employees. The advice given by Hartford Fire Insurance legal counsel, Diana Rousseau Belbruno, is to have every job candidate sign a release with the application for employment; contact all prior employers, providing them with a copy of the release; check the applicant's references; and conduct other pertinent checks such as credit. She does caution, however, that if conducting a credit check, the Fair Credit Reporting Act and numerous state laws require employers to notify applicants in writing that an investigative consumer report may be made, including information as to character, general reputation, personal characteristics, and mode of living. Furthermore, if the information obtained in the credit check is the basis upon which employment is denied, the employer is required to provide the applicant with the name and address of the agency providing the report. Another important clause to include in pre-employment screening processes is that the offer of employment is contingent upon satisfactory completion of the investigation.

According to a study conducted by one of the leading pre-employment agencies, John E. Reid and Associates, an applicant's attitude with regard to honesty is not necessarily a predictor of the individual's future behavior. The study also concluded that a job applicant with a "poor attitude toward honesty" is not any more likely to engage in acts of misconduct than those applicants rated more favorably. However, what did appear to be a valid indicator of an applicant's future behavior was an evaluation of their past work and personal behavior. The individual's performance in prior employment positions and their relationship with peers and employers served more to predict a potential employee's future performance (*Discipline Practices in the U.S. Postal Services,* 1994).

Based upon this research and other studies conducted on pre-employment screening the data strongly supports the importance of conducting thorough background investigations on potential employees. Written examinations, however, are simply not effective nor are they designed to adequately measure an applicant's tendency to misconduct and workplace violence.

Conducting criminal checks is another problem area for many employers when conducting pre-employment screening. However, recent Supreme Court decisions appear to be reversing its trend on interpretations of Title VII Civil Rights assurances. Employers are advised to continue to place greater emphasis on conducting extensive background investigations on potential employees. It is estimated that 30 percent of all employment applications contain significant misrepresentations, such as overstated qualifications, nonexistent academic credentials, lack of work history, phony references, and a multitude of embellishments. This type of investigation involves interviewing as many past acquaintances and past employers as possible including an examination of relevant records such as criminal, employment, driving, academic, and financial.

The limitations to such a procedure are the time and cost involved in these types of screening processes. As a cost reduction measure and a preliminary elimination process to beginning an extensive background investigation, employers may think about using computerized interviews for job applicants. The research on these types of interviews have been favorable. According to *Discipline Practices in the U.S. Postal Services* (1994), computerized interviews of job applicants were more likely to develop accurate information than traditional screening methods. The researchers concluded that applicants were more likely to indicate detrimental information to a computer than an interviewer. Regardless of the preliminary pre-employment technique, an extensive background investigation should be conducted on those applicants that are in final consideration for employment. There are a multitude of resources available to assist the employer in developing an effective pre-employment screening process. Every employer should have pre-employment as part of their hiring policy, no matter which technique is used.

Disciplinary Procedures

A second policy consideration should be acts of violence/employee disciplinary procedures. Employee disciplinary procedures should be designed with the employee in mind. Employees should be made aware of any deficiencies or concerns by management as soon as they surface. The employee should be given specific and factual information regarding criticism of their performance or lack thereof. The employer's expectations should be provided to the employee and the opportunity for improvement given. The company should have clear policies that prohibit any of the following violent or disruptive behavior:

- Fighting or engaging in any violent physical contact;

- Stalking, harassing, threatening, or intimidating others with physical violence;

- Carrying firearms, explosives, ammunition, or other weapons on company property, premises under company control, or areas where employees work;

- Engaging in activity that causes damage to property of the company or of an employee or engaging in acts of sabotage.

This rule against exhibiting any of this behavior must be backed with the promise that any employee who commits an act of physical violence *will* be terminated. Discretion may be exercised for employees who engage in threatening or disruptive behavior, however, it becomes critical for corporations to develop and empower a "threat assessment team" or "emergency response team" to evaluate complaints and actual incidents. This team must have the support of management in order to be effective. Equally important is a statement in the corporate policy from those with decision-making authority that the company has a zero-tolerance policy for workplace violence and that employees who engage in or threaten violent behavior will be terminated.

Threat assessment teams have been developed at a number of fortune 500 companies including IBM. After a number of violent incidents, IBM developed such teams to investigate any and all threats of violence or actual incidents of workplace violence. The team which is made up of staff from the human resources department, security, health-and-safety, and legal departments. They claim that they have been very successful in reducing the number of potentially violent incidents.

Another organization revising their procedures for dealing with disgruntled workers is the United States Postal Service. Postmaster General Marvin T. Runyon, in a joint hearing of two House of Representatives' Post Office subcommittees and the Civil Service Committee, stated that his agency will improve its handling of disgruntled workers by instituting labor-management panels to deal with disputes. They will also implement a 24-hour hotline to report threats of violence and develop and utilize more effective screening procedures for both permanent and temporary applicants. The postal service will also be using national contract services to check the employment, criminal, and driving histories of each and every applicant (*New York Times,* 1993).

The corporate policy should also address termination procedures. Considerable thought should go into any downsizing and layoffs as well as the termination of an employee. Based upon this research and that of others, the disgruntled employee represents the greatest risk for workplace violence. Therefore, termination, disciplinary measures, or layoffs must be sensitive to the needs of those who will be affected. This means giving workers as much advance notice as possible, handling layoffs fairly and providing reasonable severance benefits if feasible. For example, Douglas Aircraft company gives every worker 60 days notice before layoffs and allows employees to take time off for job interviewing during those 60 days.

Terminated employees should be dealt with in the most humane way possible. Personal anger should not enter into the situation and the person conducting the termination interview should not be cold or impersonal while dealing with the employee. Management should demonstrate a sincere interest in the welfare of the terminated employee and should consider severance benefits, out-placement benefits, and retraining, when appropriate. Terminations should take place at the beginning or end of the shift, the employee should not be permitted to return to the workplace, all company identification and keys should be retrieved, and, if a violent reaction is anticipated, security personnel should be readily available (Kaufer, 1992).

Human resource directors must be prepared to work with managers and supervisors to address the problem constructively. Steps that can be taken include:

1. tactfully approaching employees suspected of being abuse victims, encouraging them to look at their situations and emphasizing the availability and importance of getting help;

2. offering protection on the job by screening telephone calls when appropriate and alerting the security staff to the possibility of intrusion by the abuser;

3. establishing a liaison with the local domestic violence shelter;

4. being aware of resources that will acquaint battered employees with their recourse through the criminal justice system; and

5. ensuring a workplace free of references that perpetuate stereotypes of abused women (Model, 1993).

Emergency Preparedness Plans

Emergency Preparedness Plans are critical to the effective management of a workplace violence incident. The development of an emergency preparedness plan can and should involve employees from several different areas. The plan should include such things as charts of company officials to be contacted in the event of an emergency, evacuations plans, telephone numbers for building security, medical staff, and local hospitals, and the appointment of employees in each area to coordinate activities in case of emergency.

Employers should establish procedures, detailed in the plan, for employees to follow in circumstances such as bomb threats, employees or others with weapons, or verbal threats of violence. A checklist can be developed for threats received over the phone. Most threatening situations, especially those of immediate threats, will need intervention from trained professionals such as the company or building security or the local police department.

Advanced planning, written procedures, and training of those affecting the separation can avert most possible problems. As part of a termination plan the following procedures should be followed:

1. Keys and security passes must be returned;

2. Computer passwords or special access programs must be altered;

3. All confidential materials should be accounted for;

4. Company charge cards must be returned;

5. Data system access from an employee's home computer must be blocked;

6. Card files, corporate letterhead, company vehicles, and company uniforms and badges must be accounted for;

7. All transfers of property should be witnessed and acknowledged in writing so that there will be no question afterward.

Every company regardless of size should have a written policy that states the "chain of command" for the purpose of communicating violent threats. Employees and supervisors should know who to contact in management regarding employee threats. Management should know what persons in medical or personnel could be of assistance in determining the credibility of the threats. The policy should contain specific procedures with regard to the termination of workers and handling of grievances. (See Appendix 5a for a Model Policy for Workplace Threats and Violence.)

Another important element of a emergency disaster plan is to have a section dealing specifically with what the company must do in the event of a workplace violence incident. For example, a referral policy or on-site employee assistance program (EAP) should be prepared to provide necessary support after a crisis. If an employer does not have an EAP, then local agencies or counselors should be identified and used as contacts in the event of a crisis. Depending upon the particular situation, employees can either be referred to the agency or counselor(s), or support professionals can provide on-site services. In the event of a violent event, professional emotional support must be readily and immediately available. EAP's can play critical roles in prevention and crisis management as well as provide Human Resource professionals trained in crisis management that can assist in preventive training and follow-up counseling. Employers need to be aware that there are some situations in which confidential information obtained through an EAP is required to be disclosed. These include when employers or physicians learn of an employee or client's potentially dangerous behavior that may endanger others. This is discussed more in-depth in Chapter 6: "The Aftermath of Lethal Workplace Violence."

Behavioral scientists propose that employees who are unprepared and untrained to recognize potentially violent persons appear to be at greater risk. The employer has an obligation to make employees aware of potential hazards in the workplace that could result in a workplace violence incident, and how they can protect themselves and their co-workers.

A program that appears to be effective against lethal workplace violence is one developed by Linda Glasson, CHPA, Maryview Medical Center in Portsmouth, Virginia, Director of Safety and Security. The program is RAP DEE—Recognition, Alert, Preparedness, Design, Education, and Enforcement. In the recognition phase of the process Glasson states that it is imperative that fellow employees and supervisors be able to recognize the signs and symptoms of disruptive/violent behavior. She admits that although you may or may not be able to prevent a dangerous outburst, you may be able to take steps to lessen the impact. The RAP-DEE program train staff in such topics as motor signs, attitude, posture, and speech. Great care is taken with terminated employees. Those involved in the process are instructed to watch closely for any physical telltale signs such as the clenching of facial muscles or fists. What was their demeanor, was there any eye contact? The ALERT comes when the employee or supervisor notices behavior that appears violent or potentially explosive. Security is to be alerted immediately. The program has three levels of alert: Call, Come, or Immediately. "Call" means that security is requested to call the area for more information. "Come" means come to the area, and "immediately" means an incident is occurring or about to occur.

Training topics that have been recommended by OSHA suggest that employees should be trained in knowing access and egress routes, keeping doors locked to prevent intruders from entering, notifying management about suspicious persons or activities, and other safety and security measures. For example, in the 1996 OSHA publication "Guidelines for Preventing Workplace Violence for Health Care Social Service Workers," OSHA recommends that a workplace violence training program should involve all employees, including supervisors and managers. The training should be given to new and reassigned employees as well as visiting staff.

The training program should be designed so that it incorporates role-playing, simulations, and drills. OSHA recommends that topics such as Management of Assaultive Behavior, Professional Assault Response Training, police assault avoidance programs, or personal safety training such as awareness, avoidance, and how to prevent assaults, be included.

They have developed the following workplace violence model curriculum for healthcare and social service workers:

- The workplace violence prevention policy;

- Risk factors that cause or contribute to assaults;

- Early recognition of escalating behavior or recognition of warning signs or situations that may lead to assaults;

- Ways of preventing or defusing volatile situations or aggressive behavior, managing anger, and appropriately using medications as chemical restraints;

- Information on multicultural diversity to develop sensitivity to racial and ethnic issues and differences;

- A standard response action plan for violent situations, including availability of assistance, response to alarm systems, and communication procedures;

- How to deal with hostile persons other than patients and clients, such as relatives and visitors;

- Progressive behavior control methods and safe methods of restraint application or escape;

- The location and operation of safety devices such as alarm systems, along with the required maintenance schedules and procedures;

- Ways to protect oneself and co-workers, including use of the "buddy system;"

- Policies and procedures for reporting and recordkeeping;

- Policies and procedures for obtaining medical care, counseling, workers' compensation, or legal assistance after a violent episode or injury. (OSHA, 1996)

OSHA recommends that supervisors, managers, and security personnel also receive workplace violence training in dealing with employees and recognizing hazardous situations. Security personnel also need threat assessment skills and training in the psychological components of handling aggressive and abusive clients, types of disorders, and ways to handle aggression and defuse hostile situation (OSHA, 1996).

Threat Assessment

Finally the corporate workplace violence policy should address the approved method of responding to potentially violent employees. How an employer responds to potentially violent acts plays a major role in predicting what the potential outcome might be. According to the CAL/OSHA Guideline for Workplace Security if a complaint alleges a workplace security hazard that has a reasonable basis in fact, and does not represent willful harassment of the employer, the complaint is considered to be valid. When CAL/OSHA conducts inspections and evaluates employers on how well they are responding to potential violence they ask the following questions:

1. Is the inspected establishment one that is considered to be at significant risk of a Type I, II or III workplace violence event?

2. What are the physical characteristics and the work practices of the establishment that affect the security of the employees who work in the establishment?

3. Have assaults occurred in the establishment in the past? If so, how often have these assaults occurred and what was their severity?

4. What measures were taken by the employer to investigate the cause(s) of assault(s) and what corrective measures were taken by the employer to prevent other assaults?

5. What, if any, are the specific workplace security issues the employer's IIP program should address?

6. If the employer is required to address workplace security issues through the IIP Program, how effective is the employers's IIP Program in identifying and correcting workplace security hazards and in investigating workplace assaults? Does the IIP Program result in effective communication, hazard assessment, hazard correction, and supervisory and employee training?

A proactive approach to reduce and hopefully prevent workplace violence would be to form a crisis management team that should consist of an EAP counselor, management representatives, first line supervisors, security, law enforcement, legal representatives, union officials, and safety personnel. The team would evaluate all threats of workplace violence, determine their validity, and examine available options such as counseling or personnel action (see Appendix 5b).

Threat assessment is absolutely necessary for the particular individual assailant and consists of the following tasks: assessing the employee, determining the threat, and evaluating the risk. An example of proactive measures taken by the U.S. Postal Service include holding focus groups with employers to encourage employee input and increase feelings of control. They have also been hiring more managers with advanced communication skills (Solomon & King, 1993). To reduce employee exposure to violence by other employees, a written policy should be in place that states the chain of command for the purpose of communicating that a violent threat has been made. Employers and supervisors must know how to expediently contact management regarding employee threats (see Appendix 5c).

PRACTICE EXERCISE FOR CHAPTER 5

The intent of the practice exercises is to encourage the reader to use critical thinking skills in planning for and possibly preventing incidents of workplace violence. Often there are no right or wrong answers because each situation is different depending on the workplace setting and the individuals involved. The reader has different levels of information available as he/she proceeds through the text; however, each exercise should be attempted given the current information available. After reading the remainder of the text, the reader might choose to come back to earlier exercises and examine the answers to see if he/she would change them in light of added information.

The following exercise focuses on the experiences of the organization when two ex-employees react with lethal violence. The reader is asked to develop a plan for preventing further such incidents.

Violence Catches Company Unprepared

Prior to the 1980s most companies did not have threat management plans for dealing with workplace violence. Such was the case with a major computer manufacturing corporation that was forced by two shocking incidents to develop the full corporate workplace violence program that is now in place.

The first event involved an employee who had been fired from the company some years before. Nobody understands why, after so many years, the employee decided to re-focus his unhappiness on the company. However, one day he got into his car and drove to his old building. He drove the car up onto the sidewalk and into the lobby, jumped out, and shot and killed a security guard. He shot at a few others, killing two, and then ran upstairs and began shooting randomly. He remained in the building some six or seven hours, essentially holding all the employees hostage while SWAT teams and other negotiators talked with him. (Eventually, he surrendered. He was tried and convicted, and he committed suicide in prison sometime later.)

Although company management could scarcely believe that this could be more than an isolated event, they rushed to put together emergency plans throughout the company. Officials and employees alike were stunned when only three months later a second incident occurred at another location. This person had just been fired and had a particular grudge against the company department which he believed was responsible for his termination.

Many changes were initiated as a result of both these cases. Examples of defensive changes were: extending the protective perimeter by preventing cars from driving up to the building, hardening lobbies by creating a second barrier within the lobby, installing alarms, providing building maps, and putting special telephones in place for use in hostage negotiations.

The company has asked you, an outside consultant, to help them develop their Workplace Violence Policy and prepare contingency plans to prevent such an incident from happening in the future.

Developing a Workplace Violence Policy and Plan

1. Develop a corporate statement regarding your company's position on workplace violence: i.e., The XYZ Corporation will not tolerate acts of violence, threats or intimidation of violence, discrimination, or lack of respect towards other employees.

_____

_____

_____

_____

_____

2. List what types of behaviors would be prohibited conduct.

_____

_____

_____

3. Indicate the outcome for an employee who commits an act of violence against another in the workplace.

_____

_____

_____

_____

4. Create a "Violence Task Force" to address specific areas needed in implementing a Workplace Violence Policy. For example, what departments should be on the Task Force and what would their responsibilities be?

_____

_____

_____

_____

_____

5. Develop at least six Task Force objectives, i.e., analysis of high-risk areas.

_____

_____

_____

_____

_____

_____

6.   Develop a Prevention and Emergency Response Plan that contains the following elements:

- Training in recognizing and responding to workplace violence or threats;

- Increased security of XYZ's premises;

- Coordination with local police authorities on prevention and response to incidents;

- Resort to the legal process to protect employees and property;

- Prevention, incident, and post-incident responsibilities for functional areas.

6   The Aftermath of Lethal Workplace Violence

The minutes, hours, and days following a lethal workplace violence incident are critical to the survival of an organization. Attention should be directed in two areas: first, the employees who were directly affected and were victims of the incident, to their families, and also to the employees who may have been indirectly affected. The second area needing immediate attention is the organization and its ability to recover as quickly as possible from the incident.

Often, for victims of violent crime, the attack is just the beginning of their ordeal. Survivors of violent crimes often suffer from depression, anxiety, and physical complaints unrelated to the attack. Some studies have shown that up to one-half of rape victims examined recover on their own. However, 35 percent of the victims of violent crimes develop post-traumatic stress disorder. The intensity of the victims' reactions are often too much for the victim and his/her friends and family to deal with effectively. While some can and will recover without any formal treatment, others will require professional help to cope with their reactions.

Post-traumatic stress disorder, (PTSD) is a clinical diagnostic term used to describe a set of reactions that follow one or more traumatizing events. The difference between PTSD and temporary post-traumatic stress is that post-traumatic stress is a temporary condition often asso-ciated with violent incidents. PTSD is described as a long-term condi-tion. Employees who suffer from any level of post-traumatic stress have a number of recognizable symptoms such as recurring bad dreams, severe depression, anxiety, and feelings of guilt.

Employees may react differently in dealing with a traumatic event and its aftermath. The greater a person's mental strength and psyche, the more capable they are at dealing with and overcoming traumatic events. Traumatic events often eliminate the illusion employees have that something like this could never happen to them. The result is that many employees will become more guarded and vigilant and yet still feel unsafe. Over time, this condition usually passes; if it does not, the increased stress levels can do serious physical and psychological damage to the individual. Avoiding or denying the emotions that accompany a traumatic event can add to their effect on the individ-ual. It is important that they confront and deal with these feelings.

The most important area to focus on is the incident itself, both in prevention and in aftercare for survivors. Security measures and more open communications between levels of the organization can help to prevent violence in the workplace. Once a violent act occurs, addi-tional actions may be warranted. A rapid response team/program is essential to help the survivors cope with the violence.

Post-incident response and evaluation are essential to an effective violence prevention program. Companies should develop a post-inci-dent response plan (PIR). The plan should cover everything from debriefing personnel to assisting them with emotional problems resulting from the incident, with the intent of bringing closure to the incident.

More specifically the plan should include procedures for the for-mation of a workplace violence trauma team which is essential to help survivors cope with the violence. The team would be responsi-ble for implementing the plan immediately following an incident. The plan should provide a debriefing 24 to 72 hours after a serious inci-dent of violence to include all effected employees so that the cause of the violence and expectations can be discussed. A plan of action should be addressed, and those needing further counseling can be identified. A group debriefing may be necessary for immediate co-workers in how to communicate with the victims or their co-workers who are re-entering the job after an absence post-incident. Procedures for notifying police and the families of victims should be developed. The logistics of providing access for emergency services, law enforcement and essential personnel to the site should be identified.

Pre-planning proved beneficial for one manufacturing company on the West Coast with more than 300,000 employees when it experienced a workplace violence incident. An employee shot his lover and wounded another individual before turning the gun fatally on himself. This incident occurred at a plant where training had recently been conducted and an action plan developed. Although, in this particular case, the death and injury probably could not have been prevented, at least the planned system for coping with the aftermath worked flawlessly. Police were immediately on the scene, next of kin were promptly informed, press releases were written, and the plant closed temporarily—during which time employees and relatives were counseled.

This plan should be designed just like that of any emergency disaster plan with a section on responding to workplace violence incidents. The plan should include such things as:

- Designating a threat management team;

- Providing guidance concerning liaison with outside assistance;

- Providing guidance developed in concert with local authorities for collecting and preserving evidence, including interview of involved parties;

- Managing of communications regarding the incident, for example, media relations, internal communications, and possible use of a rumor control desk;

- Managing the release of sensitive information where appropriate;

- Assigning responsibilities for contacting the families of victims;

- Managing clean-up and repairs;

- Making decisions about returning to work;

- Notifying customers and suppliers about changes in orders;

- Providing employees and their families with information about their benefits; and

- Managing operations and trauma care after the crisis.

The threat management team is a critical component of every successful threat management plan. Other elements that should be included in the plan that focus on the survivors of a workplace violence incident include:

- Providing a 24-hour hotline;

- Small support group meetings;

- Health care assistance to include handling of medical insurance claims;

- Procedures for dealing with the press;

- Telephone teams to advise employees on when to return to work;

- Clean-up procedures to remove all traces of the incident;

- How orders and deliveries will be handled;

- Notify the trauma team, which should have already been selected with the assistance of your EAP personnel.

According to a survey conducted by the Society for Human Resources Management (SHRM) of 479 human resource professionals, 41 percent of the respondents reported increased stress in the workplace after violent incidents, with almost 20 percent reporting paranoia, and 18 percent reporting an increase in distrust among employees. Anger was also more pronounced according to 14 percent of the respondents and decreased productivity was reported by 12 percent (Losey, 1994).

Another study conducted in 1991 by the Barrington Psychiatric Institute in Los Angeles also supports the importance of responding immediately following an incident of workplace violence. The study used 200 people who were suffering from major psychic trauma and divided them into two groups. One group was given therapy immediately, and the other half began at a later date. The results indicated that the first group averaged 12 weeks to recovery time before returning to work. Only 13 percent of them chose to pursue litigation. The second group averaged 46 weeks of recovery time, and 94 percent chose litigation (Bensimon, 1994).

For a manufacturer of power electronics equipment in San Diego, California, management relied heavily upon employee counseling and therapy after a laid-off production test technician killed two executives and injured numerous others. The company turned to their employee assistance coordinator to assemble a trauma team. The team consisted of psychotherapists from diverse backgrounds: male and female, Caucasian and Asian, psychologists and psychiatrists. Employers provided their employees with two weeks of therapy, which was available 24 hours a day and individual, as well as group debriefing sessions. Therapists were also available, at the employees' request, to meet with their family members to help them deal with their anxiety due to their loved one returning to work. For those employees who were unable to return to work immediately, telephone therapy was available.

Although reduced work productivity is often associated with a workplace violence incident, this manufacturing company was still able to meet its production deadlines. The therapy did not interfere with the production schedule and provided management with some useful insight for dealing with potential problems in the future. For example they learned that they needed to have a more open line of communication between the employees and management. The result was implementing an employee suggestion system with the assistance of comment boxes throughout the plant. These suggestions or comments would then be brought up anonymously at employee meetings.

Companies' responses to workplace violence have been somewhat of a trial and error process. For example, a financial institution in Maryland added various physical security measures including metal detectors and additional security officers. Interestingly, the security officers were well received by the employees but the introduction of the metal detectors was viewed as excessive. The bank also made some physical changes to the office space by removing all the high wall cubicles and replacing them with lower walls permitting employees to see others around them. According to banking officials, the most calming and well-received action was for management to become more visible at the employees' work stations and throughout the office area rather than in their offices.

The company also made several physical security changes such as adding a mechanized identification card system for employees and requiring that both employees and visitors wear badges. They also installed an emergency warning system that will work independent of their communications system. The communications system had been disabled when the disgruntled employee shot out the switchboard.

The company also developed the policy of providing outplacement services for employees that were laid off and make psychological assistance available to help employees deal with the trauma of termination. Finally, the biggest lesson learned by this company was to have a trauma plan in place ahead of time, and copies available at off-site locations. That, in addition to natural disaster plans, should cover man-made traumas as well.

Case Study

The following case study provides a detailed look at how one agency responded in the aftermath of a workplace violence incident. The U.S. Postal Service learned by focusing on the needs of the employees and their families that they were able to recover quickly from a workplace violence incident. They also learned the importance of having a post-incident response plan in dealing with the myriad of details that follow an incident of this nature.

This case study, prepared by Robert W. Fisher of the United States Postal Service, outlines the United States Postal Service response to an incident of workplace violence that occurred at the Royal Oak, Michigan Post Office in November of 1991. (Mr. Fisher is Customer Service and Sales Manager for the Northland District of the United States Postal Service.)

On Thursday morning, November 14, 1991, a former letter carrier, who was officially terminated the day before, walked in the back door of the Royal Oak, Michigan, Main Post Office and began shooting. When police were finally able to enter the building they found the gunman had killed four Royal Oak postal employees, left four others injured, and then took his own life.

Mr. Fisher, who was appointed temporary Manager/Postmaster for the Royal Oak Management Sectional Center, had three objectives: evaluate the situation, establish control, and begin the healing process so the office could regain a sense of normalcy.

At 5:00 p.m. on Friday, November 15, Mr. Fisher began the process of dealing with the aftermath of a workplace violence incident. There were apparently two underlying problems with the Royal Oak Center: there was low employee morale due to a perceived authoritarian management style, and secondly there was high customer dissatisfaction, which was attributed to service cutbacks.

Immediately following the event, like that of an earthquake, a shockwave traveled beyond the Royal Oaks Center into the community and onto several nearby post offices. Employees exhibited emotions such as anger, fear, confusion, and a deep sense of loss. Several crisis intervention organizations in the Detroit Metropolitan area begin assisting by setting up counseling centers in a public library, the YMCA and a nearby postal facility.

The next immediate concern was the victims and their families. A few hours after the shooting, human resource experts had arrived on site to work one-on-one with the relatives of the victims. Their charge was to make sure victims' needs were being met and that individuals fully understood their employee benefits.

The media arrived only simultaneously with that of medical and enforcement personnel and within a few hours after the shooting, a press release was given. Mr. Fisher emerged as the official spokesperson and recounts how one of the first newspaper articles to appear spoke of a mother who took her two children out of school right after the shooting so that they could visit the scene of the postal killings. One of the children, age 11, was quoted as saying, "I was thinking there'd be blood on the windows . . . A lot of parents wouldn't bring their kids here, but to us, it's like a field trip" (Askari, 1991).

The media, employees, and politicians were calling for Royal Oak management to take responsibility for this incident. This may have been prompted by the employee allegations in Royal Oak of an ineffective, autocratic style of management. This focused blame squarely upon management. Mr. Fisher attempted to avoid finger pointing and focused more on the issues surrounding the incident.

Another important area of concern by employees was security. Employees were very fearful of another incident like this occurring and wanted visible signs of enhanced security measures.

In the midst of all this there was the concern of providing mail service. A number of collection boxes had been eliminated, several offices in the area reduced their front lobby hours, and the consistency of mail delivery was erratic at best.

Based upon these elements Mr. Fisher decided upon two directions he would need to take. First and foremost was to emphasize the healing process and establish his personal credibility with key concerned groups, primarily employees and the media. He accomplished this by spending a lot of time with the media early on in the process and communicating to them his desire to help heal the tragedy. The result was a number of favorable news stories detailing his intentions. Mr. Fisher avoided all questions about peripheral issues like past management decisions and focused on the healing process.

Mr. Fisher began his first day at 5:30 a.m. by walking through the workroom floor and visiting with each employee in the Royal Oak Main Post Office. This was also the employees' first day back since the incident. Special attention was given that day and many subsequent days to providing counseling services to both employees and their families. Moreover, a benefits specialist was assigned to each family to help resolve any problems they had. The red tape associated with leave of absence was dispensed with especially when it came to employees attending funerals, visitations, and planned memorial services.

To deal with the issue of blame a communication specialist team was used to help bridge the gap between employees and management. A daily newsletter was published to address any topics of concern and also inform employees about funerals, memorial services, counseling, hospital updates, relief funds, paycheck distribution, and other pertinent news. Daily meetings were also scheduled with Sectional Center directors, various union leaders, and management leaders. All of these representatives were involved in decision-making on such topics as security, filling of vacancies, distribution of relief donations, media relations, and improving service. Mr. Fisher made it clear to all parties that the mission of this group was to further the healing process, improve labor/management climate and look to the future. The intent was not to find blame. Both of these actions were very successful in minimizing rumors and improving communications throughout the agency.

Because of the tremendous media attention, a special media communications team was established to handle the hundreds of calls received daily.

Once stability had been established among employees and the healing process had begun, the next area of concern needing immediate attention was customer satisfaction. Customer needs had to be addressed and services resumed. Letter carrier start times were reestablished, most of the collection boxes were put back in place, and all delayed mail was processed.

This case study provides a close look at what takes place in the aftermath of a workplace violence incident. The postal service learned some very valuable lessons from the Royal Oak incident which received national attention and was the focus of the ABC News television program 20/20 in 1992. The postal service, in preparing future post-incident response (PIR) programs, incorporate the following lessons learned from the Royal Oak shooting:

1. Identify early on a spokesperson who is also in charge of the recovery process;

2. Have ready PIR teams consisting of professionals in human relations, labor relations, and communications;

3. Communications is a critical component of a successful recovery. Talk with employees daily and keep them up-to-date with both positive and negative information. Use hard-print medium, such as newsletters, to deliver information to employees;

4. Management needs to make personal contact with employees as soon as possible following the incident. Make a point of talking with all employees throughout the process;

5. As was the case with Royal Oaks, when a number of employees are involved in the incident it is helpful to have a memorial service to help the employees and the community recover from the tragedy;

6. It is critical to have crisis intervention professionals available within hours of the incident;

7. Where possible, dispense with administrative red tape, especially when it involves benefits for families and time off for employees;

8. As soon as possible following an incident, a news release should be prepared for the media. The sooner they are provided with information by a designated official, the more accurate the coverage of the incident will be. Often this will defuse negative reporting;

9. Work with the community and allow them to assist. This will help in the healing process for both the company and the community.

In concerted efforts to understand and prevent incidents of workplace violence, researchers have limited work evaluating organizational responses, even though immediate reaction is necessary and vital to maintaining operations. By focusing efforts on both employee needs and organizational operations, administrators are less likely to suffer adverse effects from these incidents.

The importance of meeting employee needs, including employee victims, and their families and other non-victim employees, through counseling, and debriefing, for example, cannot be understated. Obviously, the organization cannot operate effectively without functional employees. Once employee needs are addressed, organizational issues, such as clean up or revaluating security polices and procedures, must be considered.

The case study emphasizes the importance of planning, which is a crucial part of effectively dealing with the aftermath of these incidents. Although recommendations have been made, there is no single plan that would suffice for every organization. Therefore, management would be well advised to use the preceding guidelines as a framework for developing individualized plans following an assessment of their organizational needs.

As serious as the problem of workplace violence is, whether recognized as a criminal justice, law enforcement, or health problem, it is incumbent upon those in key positions to address multiple components of the issue. A basic understanding of the phenomena, considerations for prevention, and dealing with aftermath are each necessary for the problem ever to be decreased or eliminated.

Practice Exercise for Chapter 6

The intent of the practice exercises is to encourage the reader to use critical thinking skills in planning for and possibly preventing incidents of workplace violence. Often there are no right or wrong answers because each situation is different depending on the workplace setting and the individuals involved. The reader has different levels of information available as he/she proceeds through the text; however, each exercise should be attempted given the current information available. After reading the remainder of the text, the reader might choose to come back to earlier exercises and examine the answers to see if he/she would change them in light of added information.

The following exercise focuses on the information needed to be prepared to deal with the aftermath of an incident of lethal workplace violence. The reader is asked to identify a set of priority action items for responding to this incident and to consider the implementation of these actions.

The Aftermath of Lethal Workplace Violence: Being Prepared

The following is a fictitious scenario based on an actual case. Your assignment is to play the role of the Human Resource Director for a large ocean cruise line, the Holiday. Before going to work this morning you were shocked to read the following article in a national newspaper. The article is about a particularly troublesome case you have been handling at Holiday.

"WHEN IS MENTAL STATE OF A CRUISE LINE CAPTAIN GROUNDS FOR GROUNDING HIM? Holiday Cruise Line is Sued After Sending Ashore a Captain Who Got Into Spats at Home and in the Bridge"

Captain Edward G. O'Brian had been commanding the Holiday for more than 20 years when, on a hot and humid afternoon in August of 1990, he lost his cool.

The large, burly former Navy SEAL, angry with his wife, threw his beer bottle against the wall, barely missing her and headed for the closet where he kept one of his many firearms. "This will all be over for both of us soon!" Frightened, Mrs. O'Brian grabbed her car keys and fled the house.

She notified police from her mobile phone and waited for their arrival before re-entering the house. Inside the house she found the police officers handcuffing her husband, who was vigorously resisting while shouting obscenities. The officers arrested Captain O'Brian and took him to jail. He was held without bond and later transferred to a locked psychiatric facility for a court-ordered evaluation.

The 52-year-old Captain O'Brian, known for his nickname as Captain Ego, spent several weeks in various psychiatric hospitals. According to a psychiatrist's notes, Mrs. O'Brian described her husband as a "rageaholic" who "has physically strong-armed me enough to bruise me" and once pulled her from the car by her hair. The captain admitted he had once been arrested for breaking the windshield of a car with his bear hands. At one point he identified himself as having a drinking problem.

Several psychiatrists diagnosed O'Brian as having a personality disorder, and a strong propensity for impulsivity and emotional outbursts. They even went so far as to imply that these outbursts could result in injury to O'Brian and others.

Should Captain O'Brian be allowed to pilot his ship again?

Although these events left Holiday Cruise Line with some doubts regarding Captain O'Brian, after months of psychiatric evaluation, Captain O'Brian resumed command of the ship. It wasn't until a serious argument on the bridge of the ship, which erupted between him and his first mate, that Holiday Cruise Lines took action to suspend him. However, the suspension did not occur immediately—it took several months.

Meanwhile, the Cruise Line Industry Association (CLIA) has certified Captain O'Brian as fit to command five times since his domestic dispute, including three since the bridge incident. Then, a year ago, it reversed itself and denied him the first-class medical certificate captains need to commandeer a ship.

Captain O'Brian is fighting to return to sea. He is suing Holiday Cruise Lines, its medical consultant, and CLIA in federal court in Miami.

In his courtroom testimony, O'Brian described how the August afternoon began over a trivial matter. Mrs. O'Brian had assured her husband that she had mailed some photos to a potential buyer of a sailboat they had restored. But when he walked into the kitchen, the photos lay on the counter.

Troubled over their finances, the captain became irate saying, "I'm going to do what Grayson did," referring to her brother, who had killed himself. In court testimony, Captain O'Brian admitted to attempting to provoke his wife. According to a doctor's notes from 1990, Captain O'Brian told him he put a gun to his head and cocked it but didn't intend to use it. In later court testimony, however, he recanted this earlier discussion with the Doctor.

During the next two days, his lawyer negotiated with prosecutors to get him out of jail and into a treatment facility in Miami. There, during exams in the psychiatric ward, he described in detail about his upbringing and early adulthood.

The son of middle-class midwestern parents, he joined the Navy at age 17 and later became a Navy SEAL. He had two tours of duty in Vietnam in which he was awarded several medals including a Navy Commendation. In 1969 he completed his apprenticeship with the Holiday Cruise Line and was given full command of a ship.

His trouble began in July of 1979 when he received a letter of reprimand for drinking before taking command of his ship. Then in 1985 he was suspended for one month when his voice, by accident, was heard over the ship's public address system shouting profanities at his crew members.

Beginning in the mid 1980s he developed some medical problems that affected his sleeping habits, which often caused him daytime drowsiness. He was put on leave for evaluation.

He was able to make some lifestyle adjustments which improved his health. Approximately two years later he was reassigned to his ship and did his job without mishap for a year and a half when the domestic dispute occurred in 1990.

At the Miami psychiatric facility, Captain O'Brian underwent an extensive evaluation. Holiday Cruise officials got involved. Suspecting alcohol abuse, they arranged to have Captain O'Brian transferred to Lighthouse Hospital, where Holiday sends alcoholic captains, and then to a third area facility, Seaview Institute.

One picture that emerges from the CLIA record of doctors' notes and testimony is a strict and dominating personality with a propensity for outbursts. He described his second marriage, which lasted for more than 10 years, as mutually violent. His second ex-wife, Susan, was once stuck in the hand with a knife during an altercation which he contends was unintentional. Susan, however, says that it was only O'Brian that was violent.

The doctors presented a wide variety of diagnoses, including "manic depression," "narcissistic personality disorder with compulsive traits," and "intermittent explosive disorder." They also identified signs of alcohol abuse which they determined was not the main problem.

The psychologist who indicated that the captain's personality might lead to some dangerous outburst, determined him to be a high suicidal risk. He added, though, that it is virtually impossible to evaluate one's potential for violence.

Along those descriptions of O'Brian, another emerged. Another psychiatrist, wrote that the captain's problems were brief and intermittent and a result of marital and financial stresses. The captain, while admitting to bouts with anger, always had explanations. He said, for example, that when he bashed the car windshield it was an accident. He was not charged for that.

He also unexpectedly declared himself an alcoholic at a group therapy session, but afterwards told doctors he did not really believe it—he just knew that captains who are recovering alcoholics are federally protected from job discrimination.

Ex-wife Susan, a former cruise director, says that despite their unstable relationship, if there was an emergency on the ship, she would want Captain O'Brian to be in command. "He's a very competent captain, and what he does at home does not affect his job performance."

A few weeks later, Captain O'Brian was released with orders to continue seeing Dr. Jones. Dr. Jones, in turn, sent him for evaluation by a clinical psychologist, who agreed the captain was fine. "He is eccentric and full of spirit, and not crazy or disabled."

His wife, who never sought to have her husband prosecuted, soon reunited with him. Prosecutors consequently reduced the charge to a misdemeanor of assault and later dismissed that. The O'Brian's resumed marriage counseling and increased their commitment to religion as born-again Christians.

In May 1990, Dr. Jones approved the captain to return to work. CLIA's chief psychiatrist recommended his health certification be restored with scheduled psychiatric updates. He described the captain as "stubborn, pompous, egotistical, dominating, pushy, and intimidating," but he found no evidence that the captain's problems had affected his job performance. In January 1991, CLIA recertified him.

This evaluation alone did not satisfy Holiday, however. It sent him to visit Dr. Parker, dreaded by most captains because of his reputation for relieving them of their duties. Dr. Parker also determined that Captain O'Brian was fit for duty. He did indicate, however, that if Captain O'Brian demonstrated any unusual behavior in the future that indicates the occurrence of an adjustment disorder, he should be permanently relieved of his duties.

Captain O'Brian was back at sea. But just six months after his return, he ran into more problems. On an assignment in the Caribbean, he and the ship's first officer, a younger man had repeated conflicts, both on the bridge and off.

The mood was set from the very beginning. The first officer reported to his superiors at Holiday that the Captain had an over-inflated ego. Moreover, he indicated that Captain O'Brian reacted hostilely when his crew tried to point out errors. He also said the captain broke through his assigned course three times.

Captain O'Brian, in his own subsequent report, said the variations in course were minimal and not a safety violation. Captain O'Brian called his crew insubordinate and said that he felt as if he were operating the ship alone.

The conflict was exacerbated in the Cayman Islands only two weeks into their cruise. The second officer's report to superiors said that Captain O'Brian had a fit of rage on the bridge.

"The Captain's terribly negative attitude along with his violent, disruptive personality make it very difficult for everyone to perform their duties," he wrote. "I'm very concerned that all of these adverse characteristics will eventually culminate in a major disaster."

In CLIA testimony, Captain O'Brian indicated that he had simply "chewed him out."

Although Captain O'Brian told his supervising director by phone of the conflict, the trip continued and was uneventful. "Looking back, I wish I had ended the cruise," the director later told CLIA.

In succeeding months, Captain O'Brian kept working as usual, though Holiday sent along monitors to check his performance. He passed. In January 1992, CLIA renewed his certificate for six months.

Company records presented in the hearing show that within Holiday, managers had largely concluded Captain O'Brian was to blame for the dispute on the bridge, and there was talk of relieving him of his duties. A meeting to resolve the conflict was held in February 1994, including the three crew members, but it turned into yet another dispute; Captain O'Brian declined a suggestion to obtain counseling.

He continued commanding the ship. Holiday again sent a monitor who reported that Captain O'Brian's performance on all occasions was very good.

Holiday then sent him back to Dr. Parker. This time he discussed the incident with Holiday managers, the ships officers, conferred with his consultants and interviewed the Captain again. Dr. Parker concluded that Captain O'Brian should not be allowed to command the ship. Dr. Parker said that he kept quoting Bible verses which had no relevance. Captain O'Brian who covertly taped the session contends the doctor's assessment was designed to relieve him. Dr. Parker denied this.

Dr. Parker concluded that the captain exhibited a "narcissistic personality disorder" which is a grandiose sense of self-importance that leads to conflict with others. This is one of several specific psychiatric conditions that under CLIA rules disqualify cruise ship captains.

In March 1992, some three months after the bridge incident, Captain O'Brian was suspended. He has since been placed on medical disability at half pay.

And Dr. Parker went a step further. He sent the captain's medical records to CLIA with a note indicating that he felt very strongly the Captain should not be sailing. He followed up with further urging to relieve him of his duties. It took until February 1993, but CLIA did revoke Captain O'Brian's medical certificate. The story doesn't end there.

In his suit against Holiday and Dr. Parker, Captain O'Brian is trying to become reinstated to his job as a captain, making about $95,000 a year along with damages. He contends that Holiday was determined to have him declared medically unfit.

Holiday and Dr. Parker say the suit has no merit. "We can't take chances when it comes to the safety of our passengers," a Holiday spokesman says, Dr. Parker, in a written response to questions, says he reported him to CLIA because he felt that it was his moral obligation.

The Captain says his four years of "sheer hell" only proves his strength and stability. "There is nothing wrong with me mentally or medically," he says. "I've been under more financial and mental stress than my tours in Vietnam, and I've still been able to remain calm."

"He's not a follower. He could be a difficult employee in terms of his personality," says one of his attorneys, citing Captain O'Brian's outspoken criticism of Holiday management. "He doesn't fit the corporate mold. Does that make him crazy and unfit to sail? I don't think so."

In August of 1995, the case was heard before a crowded Miami courtroom. The second officer said he had sought a transfer to make sure he never sailed with the captain again. But other captains attested to his skills and said they had never had a problem. Mrs. O'Brian changed much of her original story and said her husband never hit her. Dr. Jones said he believed Captain O'Brian was "caught up in the system"—that his diagnoses after the domestic dispute came under extreme conditions and then those mistaken conclusions got passed from doctor to doctor.

The judge ordered the CLIA to reissue Captain O'Brian's medical certification, ruling that his skirmishes with his wife and his crew weren't sufficient signs of a mental disorder. Writing that the incident of the Captain's Bridge was "the first and only incident of this sort in [his] otherwise exemplary record," he said that all three crew members shared blame.

You have read the article and are upset as you drive in to work. You are glad you took the time to read the paper this morning because you expect major repercussions from the article.

Upon reaching your office, your secretary informs you that corporate counsel is waiting in your office, you have already received six phone calls from different media sources wanting a statement, and the 1-800-Reservations line is being bombarded with questions from customers wanting to know if O'Brian is going to captain any of the cruises they have reserved and paid for and if O'Brian, who was the captain on their cruise, has ever been a patient at Anchor Hospital.

As you enter your office, the CEO of Holiday wants to know what, if any, workplace violence plan you have in the event Captain O'Brian is allowed to return to work. More specifically, what plan have you developed in the event that an incident occurs between O'Brian and other employees and/or customers. What post-incident plans have been developed to deal with such an event? Also, you have been told to work up a report on what changes, if any, you would recommend regarding your policies on re-instating employees who have gone through treatment and/or committed acts or threats of violence in the workplace. You have also been directed to prepare a media statement on the cruise line's position regarding this matter, as well as a statement for Reservations Staff to use regarding the concerns of customers who might call them. And oh, by the way, all the above was due on the desk of corporate counsel an hour ago.

Your Response

1. List the action items that must be addressed to complete your assignment:

———   _____

———   _____

———   _____

———   _____

2. Prioritize the action items (in #1, above) by placing the priority number on the line to the left of the action item.

3. On separate paper formally document the information that must be gathered to properly complete your assignment. Separately respond to the following for each of the action items identified above.

   a. Identify the information available to you for completing this part of the assignment.

   b. Identify the information that you need to collect.

   c. Identify the sensitive issues surrounding this part of the assignment.

   d. State how you will handle the sensitive issues in dealing with this part of the assignment.

4. Looking at your morning in hindsight, what could you have done to be better prepared to respond to the CEO's demands and what might you have been able to do to avoid them?

5. What did you learn from this exercise that you might be able to put in practice in your current or future workplace?

Appendices

Appendix 1

WORKPLACE VIOLENCE
DATA COLLECTION INSTRUMENT
INCIDENT FILE

CASE #:_____YYNNN (Enter on Master List with Offender Name)

CASE NAME: _____ (Last, First)

PLACE (CITY, STATE): _____

REGION:
    1=Northeast: CT ME MA NH NJ NY PA RI VT
    2=Midwest: IL IN IA KS MI MO MN NE ND OH SD WI
    3=South: AL AR DE DC FL GA KY LA MD MS NC OK SC TN TX VA WV
    4=West: AK AZ CA CO HA ID MT NV NM OR UT WA

DATE (OF INCIDENT): ___/___/___ MM/DD/YY

SEASON:
1=Dec-Feb	3=Jun-Aug
2=Mar-May	4=Sept-Nov

TIME (OF DAY):
    _____ (Military Time 0001-2400) [1st WP incident]
    ♦=Unknown Estimate if know period of day; Circle Estimate

SIGNIF (SIGNIFICANCE OF TIME):
0=None Indicated	4=At Change of Shift
1=At Opening	5=At Closing
2=Just after Shift Change or Opening	6=Closed
3=Just before Shift Change or Closing	

DAY OF WEEK:
  1=Mon   5=Fri
  2=Tue   6=Sat
  3=Wed   7=Sun
  4=Thur   ◆=Unknown

SITE (ORGANIZATIONAL ENVIRONMENT):
  0=Retail Sales   10=Plants/Manufacturing
  1=Hotel   11=Airlines
  2=Bank   12=Home/Apartment
  3=Restaurant   13=School
  4=Office/Building   14=Bus/Car Transportation
  5=Post Office   15=Construction
  6=Government   16=Recreation/Entertainment
  7=Medical   17=Church
  8=Warehouse   18=Military
  9=Mines   19=Other (Describe: _____)

MULT SITE (MULTIPLE SITES):
  0=No
  1=Yes

OFFENDER (NUMBER OF OFFENDERS): ____

T # KILLED (TOTAL KILLED): ____   T # INJUR (TOTAL INJURED): ____

W # KILLED (KILLED IN WP): ____   W # INJUR (INJURED IN WP): ____

KILLED/INJURED OUTSIDE WORKPLACE:
  KI # HOME (AT HOME/RESIDENCE): ____
  KI # PUB (PUBLIC PLACE): ____
  KI # ISOL (ISOLATED/SECLUDED PLACE): ____

WEAPON (USED IN WORKPLACE):
  1=Revolver   8=Arson
  2=Semi-Auto Handgun   9=Drug/Poison
  3=Semi-Auto Rifle   10=Rape
  4=Knife   11=Starvation
  5=Explosive   12=Other/Miscellaneous
  6=Hands   13=None-Threat
  7=Blunt Object   14=Shotgun

TRIANGLE (LOVE):
    0=No
    1=Yes

CRIME (COMMISSION OF OTHER CRIME):
    0=No
    1=Robbery
    2=Other

ALC/DRUG (ALCOHOL/DRUG INVOLVEMENT BY ANY ASSAILANT):
    0=No
    1=Yes

JOBACT (Happened during or immediately following a job action or evaluation):

0=No	2=Don't Know
1=Yes	3=Not Applicable

H-MURDER (Murder for Hire):
    0=No
    1=Yes

Appendix 2

WORKPLACE VIOLENCE
DATA COLLECTION INSTRUMENT
OFFENDER FILE

CASE #: _____ (SAME AS FOR INCIDENT FILE)

OFFENDER'S #: ____ of _____

OFFENDER'S NAME: _____ (Last, First)

O-INJURY:

0=None	4=Serious Self-Inflicted Injury
1=Killed Self	5=Minor Self-Inflicted Injury
2=Killed by Police	6=Serious Other-Inflicted Injury
3=Killed by Other than Police or Self	7=Minor Other-Inflicted Injury

O-RELATE (OFFENDER'S POSITION IN ORGANIZATION):

0=None	5=Owner/Pres
1=Manager	6=Ex-Manager
2=Employee	7=Ex-Employee
3=Customer	8=Relative of Employee
4=Romantic involvement w/ organization employee	9=Union Official

O-TIME:
    0=Not Employee
    1=Part-Time
    2=Full-time

MOTIVE:

- 0=Unknown
- 1=Disgruntled Employee
- 2=Angry w/Employer—Retaliation/ Revenge
- 3=Fired
- 4=Romantic Rejection
- 5=Domestic Problems
- 6=Robbery
- 7=Anger over Unemployment
- 8=Hate Crime
- 9=Accident
- 10=Money from Insurance
- 11=Psychiatric Problems
- 12=Suicide
- 13=Crime Spree
- 14=Rape
- 15=Self-Defense
- 16=Strike
- 17=Frustration—Teasing/Name-Calling/Bad Treatment by Peers
- 18=Passed Over for Promotion
- 19=Suspended/Other Disciplinary Action Short of Firing
- 20=Other _____
- 21=Fear of Firing or Discipline
- 22=Disgruntled Customer

CJ STATUS:

- 0=Unknown
- 1=Died Without Trial
- 2=Not Apprehended
- 3=Jail
- 4=Death Penalty/Appeal
- 5=Acquitted
- 6=Life in Prison/20+ years, Long Sentence
- 7=Fined
- 8=Counseling
- 9=Released on Bond
- 10=Probation
- 11=Executed
- 12=Charged/Arrested
- 13=Other _____
- 14=Paroled
- 15=Prison

CHARGE:

- 0=Deceased
- 1=Murder
- 2=Negligent Homicide
- 3=Assault
- 4=Unknown
- 5=Other _____

SENTENCE:

- _____ (Yrs)
- 0=Not Applicable
- 98=Death Penalty
- 99=Life Imprisonment

AGE: _____

GENDER:

- 1=Male
- 2=Female
- 3=Unknown

RACE:
    1=White
    2=Nonwhite
    3=Unknown

MARITAL:
    1=Married   4=Single
    2=Divorced   5=Unknown
    3=Separated

CHILDREN (Number of): ____

ALC/DRUG (AT TIME OF INCIDENT):
    0=No
    1=Yes

MILITARY:
    0=No   4=AF
    1=Army   5=Unknown
    2=Marine   6=Coast Guard
    3=Navy

DISCHARG (DISCHARGE):
    0=N/A   4=Still Serving in Military
    1=Honorable   5=Less than Honorable
    2=Dishonorable   6=Medical
    3=Unknown

MILSTATUS:
    0=N/A   3=Nat Guard
    1=Active Duty   4=Unknown
    2=Reserves

VIETNAM (SERVICE):
    0=No   2=Don't Know
    1=Yes   3=N/A

SPFORCES (IN SPECIAL FORCES):
    0=No   2=Don't Know
    1=Yes   3=N/A

OCCUPATION:
    0=Unknown   2=Skilled
    1=White Collar   3=Unskilled

WORKHIST (PAST WORK HISTORY):
    0=Unknown
    1=Good
    2=Problematic

P-FIRED (FIRED FROM PRIOR JOBS):
    0=No
    1=Yes
    2=Don't Know

P-VIOL (PREVIOUS VIOLENCE):
    0=No
    1=Yes
    2=Don't Know

VIOLENT (AS DESCRIBED BY OTHERS):
    0=No
    1=Yes
    2=Don't Know

FEARED (BY OTHERS):
    0=No
    1=Yes
    2=Don't Know

P-THREAT (THREATENED VIOLENCE):
    0=No
    1=Yes
    2=Don't Know

REPORTED (THREATS, FEARS, OR VIOLENCE REPORTED
TO MANAGEMENT PRIOR TO THIS INCIDENT):
    0=No   2=Don't Know
    1=Yes   3=N/A

ACTION (MGT TOOK ACTION ON REPORTS):
    0=No   2=Unknown
    1=Yes   3=N/A

P-ARREST (ARRESTED PREVIOUSLY):
  0=No
  1=Yes
  2=Don't Know

PSYCHIAT (PSYCHIATRIC HISTORY):
  0=No
  1=Yes
  2=Don't Know

LONER:
  0=No
  1=Yes
  2=Don't Know

CITIZEN (OF U.S.):
  0=No
  1=Yes
  2=Don't Know

Appendix 3

WORKPLACE VIOLENCE
DATA COLLECTION INSTRUMENT
VICTIM FILE

CASE #: _____ (SAME AS FOR INCIDENT FILE)

VICTIM #: _____ of _____(#)

VICT NAME: _____ (Last, First)

V-INJURY:

0=Threat	2=Serious Injury
1=Killed	3=Minor Injury Only

W-RELATE (WORK RELATIONSHIP OF VICTIM TO ASSAILANT):

0=No Work Relationship	7=Other _____
1=Boss	8=Co-Owner
2=Higher Level Manager	9=Ex-Subordinate
3=Co-Worker	10=Ex-Boss
4=Subordinate	11=Ex-Co-Worker
5=Administrator/Manager Outside Assailant's Chain of Command	12=Ex-Partner
6=Manager of Unknown Relationship to Assailant	

I-RELATE (INTIMATE RELATIONSHIP OF VICTIM TO ASSAILANT):

0=None	7=Was Sought as Lover
1=Spouse	8=Rival
2=Ex-Spouse	9=Child
3=Live-In Lover	10=Other Family Member
4=Ex-Lover	11=Friend
5=Dating Partner	12=Other _____
6=Ex-Dating Partner	13=Step/Dating Child etc.

O-RELATE (VICTIM'S POSITION IN ORGANIZATION):

0=None   5=Security
1=Manager   6=Police
2=Employee   7=Ex-Manager
3=Customer   8=Ex-Employee
4=Owner/President

CONFLICT (VICTIM'S PRIOR CONFLICT WITH THE ASSAILANT):

0=None   5=Labor Mediator
1=Fired   6=Argued With
2=Disciplined   7=Property Dispute
3=Refused Romantic Advances   8=Other _____
4=Counseled Assailant to Change
     Behavior

AGE: _____

GENDER:

1=Male
2=Female
3=Unknown

RACE:

1=White
2=Nonwhite
3=Unknown

MARITAL:

1=Married   4=Single
2=Divorced   5=Unknown
3=Separated

CHILDREN (Number of): ____

PREGNANT:

0=No
1=Yes
2=N/A (Male or Gender Unknown select "N/A")
          (Female, if not known whether pregnant, select "No")

NOTES:

Appendix 4a
LATE NIGHT RETAIL VIOLENCE PREVENTION CHECKLIST

Pre-Event Measures

Make your store unattractive to robbers by:

- ❑ Removing clutter, obstructions, and signs from the windows so that an unobstructed view of the store counter and/or cash register exists.

- ❑ Keeping the store and parking lot as brightly lit as local law allows.

- ❑ Keep an eye on what is going on outside the store and report any suspicious persons or activities to the police.

- ❑ When there are no customers in the store, keep yourself busy with other tasks away from the cash register.

- ❑ Post emergency police and fire department numbers and the store's address by the phone.

- ❑ Mount mirrors on the ceiling to help you keep an eye on hidden corners of the store. Consider surveillance cameras to record what goes on in the store and to act as a deterrent.

- ❑ Post signs that are easy to spot from the outside of the store that inform customers that you have a limited amount of cash on hand.

- ❑ Limit accessible cash to a small amount and keep only small bills in the cash register.

- ❑ Use a time access safe for larger bills and deposit them as they are received.

❑   Use only one register after dark and leave unused registers open with empty cash drawers tilted up for all to see.

❑   Let your customers know that you keep only a small amount of cash on hand.

Event Measures

❑   If you are robbed at gunpoint, stay calm and speak to the robber in a cooperative tone. Do not argue or fight with the robber and offer no resistance whatsoever. Hand over the money.

❑   Never pull a weapon during the event—it will only increase your chances of getting hurt.

❑   Always move slowly and explain each move to the robber before you make it.

Post-Event Measures

❑   Make no attempt to follow or chase the robber.

❑   Stay where you are until you are certain the robber has left the immediate area, then lock the door of your store and call the police immediately.

❑   Do not touch anything the robber has handled.

❑   Write down everything you remember about the robber and the robbery while you wait for the police to arrive.

❑   Do not open the door of the store until the police arrive.

Excerpted from: CAL/OSHA *Guidelines for Workplace Security* (1995, March). Department of Industrial Relations. San Francisco, CA: Division of Occupational Safety and Health.

Appendix 4b
RECOGNIZING INAPPROPRIATE BEHAVIOR

Inappropriate behavior is often a warning sign of potential hostility or violence. When left unchecked it can escalate to higher levels. Employees who exhibit the following behaviors should be reported and disciplined in accordance with your company policy:

- Unwelcome name-calling, obscene language, and other abusive behavior.

- Intimidation through direct or veiled verbal threats.

- Throwing objects in the workplace regardless of the size or type of object being thrown or whether a person is the target of a thrown object.

- Physically touching another employee in an intimidating, malicious, or sexually harassing manner. This includes such acts as hitting, slapping, poking, kicking, pinching, grabbing, and pushing.

- Physically intimidating others including such acts as obscene gestures, "getting in your face," and fist-shaking.

Appendix 4c

WARNING SIGNS
OF POTENTIALLY
VIOLENT INDIVIDUALS

There is no exact method to predict when a person will become violent. One or more of these warning signs may be displayed before a person becomes violent but does not necessarily indicate that an individual will become violent. A display of these signs should trigger concern as they are usually exhibited by people experiencing problems:

- Irrational beliefs and ideas
- Verbal, nonverbal, or written threats or intimidation
- Fascination with weaponry and/or acts of violence
- Expressions of a plan to hurt oneself or others
- Externalization of blame
- Un-reciprocated romantic obsession
- Taking up much of supervisor's time with behavior or performance problems
- Fear reaction among co-workers/clients
- Drastic change in belief systems
- Displays of unwarranted anger
- New or increased source of stress at home or work
- Inability to take criticism
- Feelings of being victimized
- Intoxication from alcohol or other substances
- Expressions of hopelessness or heightened anxiety
- Productivity and/or attendance problems
- Violence towards inanimate objects
- Steals or sabotages projects or equipment
- Lack of concern for the safety of others

Appendix 4d

PERSONAL CONDUCT
TO MINIMIZE VIOLENCE

Follow these suggestions in your daily interactions with people to de-escalate potentially violent situations. Disengage if, at any time, a person's behavior starts to escalate beyond your comfort zone.

Do . . .

- Project calmness: move and speak slowly, quietly, and confidently.

- Be an empathetic listener: encourage the person to talk, and listen patiently.

- Focus your attention on the other person to let him or her know you are interested in what he or she has to say.

- Maintain a relaxed yet attentive posture and position yourself at a right angle rather than directly in front of the other person.

- Acknowledge the person's feelings. Indicate that you can see he or she is upset. Ask for small, specific favors such as asking the person to move to a quieter area.

- Establish ground rules if unreasonable behavior persists. Calmly describe the consequences of any violent behavior.

- Use delaying tactics that will give the person time to calm down. For example, offer a drink of water (in a disposable cup).

- Be reassuring and point out choices. Break big problems into smaller, more manageable problems.

- Accept criticism in a positive way. When a complaint might be true, use statements like "You're probably right" or "It was my fault." If the criticism seems unwarranted, ask clarifying questions.

- Ask for the individual's recommendations. Repeat back to the individual what you feel he or she is requesting of you.

- Arrange yourself so that a visitor cannot block your access to any exit.

Do Not . . .

- Use styles of communication that create hostility such as apathy, brush off, coldness, condescension, robotism, going strictly by the rules, or giving the run-around.

- Reject all of a client's demands from the start.

- Pose in challenging stances such as standing directly opposite someone with your hands on your hips or crossing your arms.

- Make any physical contact, or use finger-pointing or long periods of fixed eye contact.

- Make sudden movements that can be seen as threatening. Notice the tone, volume, and rate of your speech.

- Challenge, threaten, or dare the individual. Never belittle the person or make him/her feel foolish.

- Criticize or act impatiently toward the agitated individual.

- Attempt to bargain with a threatening individual.

- Try to make the situation seem less serious than it is.

- Make false statements or promises you cannot keep.

- Try to impart a lot of technical or complicated information when emotions are high.

- Take sides or agree with distortions.

- Invade the individual's personal space. Make sure there is a space of 3' to 6' between you and the person.

Appendix 4e

SOURCES OF WORKPLACE
VIOLENCE PREVENTION

1. For information regarding a wide variety of topics, including violence issues and delinquency prevention, contact the:

    National Criminal Justice Reference Service
    Box 6000
    Rockville, MD 20850
    Tel. (800) 851-3420
    Fax (301) 251-5212
    E-mail: askncjrs@aspensys.com
    World Wide Web site at:
    http://hicjrs.aspensys.com:81/ncjrshome.html

2. For listings of violence prevention and treatment programs available to the public, topical database searches, information on violence-related curricula and videos, etc., contact the:

    Center for the Study and Prevention of Violence
    University of Colorado at Boulder
    Institute of Behavioral Science
    Campus Box 442
    Boulder, CO 80309-0442
    Tel. (303) 492-1032
    E-mail: IBS@Colorado.edu

3. The IACP sponsors a number of publications concerning topical crime prevention issues such as combating drug crimes in the workplace.

    The International Association of Chiefs of Police
    515 N. Washington St.
    Alexandria, VA 22314-2357

Appendix 5a

MODEL POLICY FOR WORKPLACE
THREATS AND VIOLENCE

Nothing is more important to [COMPANY NAME] than the safety and security of its employees. Threats, threatening behavior, or acts of violence against employees, visitors, guests, or other individuals by anyone on [COMPANY NAME] property will not be tolerated. Violations of this policy will lead to disciplinary action which may include dismissal, arrest, and prosecution.

Any person who makes substantial threats, exhibits threatening behavior, or engages in violent acts on [COMPANY NAME] property shall be removed from the premises as quickly as safety permits, and shall remain off [COMPANY NAME] premises pending the outcome of an investigation. [COMPANY NAME] will initiate an appropriate response. This response may include, but is not limited to, suspension and/or termination of any business relationship, reassignment of job duties, suspension or termination of employment, and/or criminal prosection of the person or persons involved.

No existing [COMPANY NAME] policy, practice, or procedure should be interpreted to prohibit decisions designed to prevent a threat from being carried out, a violent act from occurring or a life-threatening situation from developing.

All [COMPANY NAME] personnel are responsible for notifying the management representative designated below of any threats which they have witnessed, received, or have been told that another person has witnessed or received. Even without an actual threat, personnel should also report any behavior they have witnessed which they regard as threatening or violent, when that behavior is job related or might be carried out on a company controlled site, or is connected to company employment. Employees are responsible for making this report regardless of the relationship between the individual who initiated the threat or threatening behavior and the person or persons who were threatened or were the focus of the threatening behavior. If the designated management representative is not available, personnel should report the threat to their supervisor or another member of the management team.

All individuals who apply for or obtain a protective or restraining order which lists company locations as being protected areas, must provide to the designated management representative a copy of the petition and declarations used to seek the order, a copy of any temporary protective or restraining order which is granted, and a copy of any protective or restraining order which is made permanent.

[COMPANY NAME] understands the sensitivity of the information requested and has developed confidentiality procedures which recognize and respect the privacy of the reporting employee(s).

The designated management representative is:

Name: _____

Title: _____

Department: _____

Telephone: _____

Location: _____

Appendix 5b

WORKPLACE VIOLENCE: PREVENTION AND EMERGENCY RESPONSE PLAN

Prepared for The Garland Equipment Agency (GEA) by the GEA Compliance Review Board

Emergency Response Team (ERT) Formation

The GEA Compliance Review Board has adopted a workplace violence prevention and response plan. A critical element of this plan is the requirement that each GEA facility create an ERT to implement the plan at their respective locations.

The Appliance Park ERT will also serve as the Business Resource for other facility ERTs. The Appliance Park ERT shall consist of:

- The plant/site manager
- Senior Counsel
- Medical Director
- Human Resources
- Manager, Communications
- Manager, Facilities
- EAP

Each satellite/major location will have its own ERT which shall consist of representatives from each of the following functions/organizations:

- Plant/site manager
- Human Resources
- Union (if applicable)
- EHS
- Security
- Medical

Field Organizations:

- Because of the size and disbursement of personnel, field organizations must prepare differently. Each field site manager should establish contact with the local police authority to determine what support is available and what procedures to follow in the event of an emergency.
- If an event occurs, the field site manager must alert:
  - The Area Relations Manager
  - The Business Resource (the AP ERT)

Emergency Response Team (ERT)

The ERT is responsible for the full implementation of the GEA Workplace Violence Policy. Each functional representative is responsible for seeing that the necessary resources are made available to the ERT from their respective functional area.

Prevention Responsibilities:

- Oversee full implementation of the GEA Workplace Violence Policy. This includes implementing all aspects of this Prevention and Emergency Response Plan.
- Assure GEA Workplace Violence Policy is applied consistently.
- If a threat is made on the life of an employee or to the security of the plant, the ERT will discuss the seriousness of the threat, the appropriate action to take, and the ramifications of the action. An investigation may be necessary. The ERT is the decisionmaker behind the policy.

Incident Responsibilities:

- The ERT must react instantly to a violent situation. For this reason, it should be one of the first notified if an incident does occur.
- Assure that all appropriate actions are taken.
- Keep the situation as organized and as calm as possible.
- Handle any problems as they occur.

Post-Incident Responsibilities:

- Assure all post-incident actions are taken by the respective functional areas as outlined in this plan.
- Review the incident
  - Were the actions taken appropriate?
  - Did the ERT react quickly enough?
  - Did the functional areas carry out their responsibilities?
  - What actions would have been better?

Training

All GEA employees will receive the appropriate level of training as follows:

- All GEA employees will receive a newsletter explaining:
  - GEA Policy on Workplace Violence
  - Awareness of Warning Signs
  - Knowledge of Notification Process—Who to Call and When
  - Knowledge of Existing Facilities such as EAP and Medical
- HR personnel, Stewards, ERT, Coordinators, BTLs, Security Personnel, and volunteers from the union hall will receive additional training:
  - More In-Depth Knowledge of the Warning Signs and Notification Process
  - Training on When and How to Refer Someone to EAP
  - Training on How to Handle Complaints, Discipline, and Dismissals
  - Training on How to Manage a Situation When it Occurs (i.e., Conflict Resolution Training)
- Technicians:
  - These employees face a unique situation by being in direct contact with consumers. For this reason, they should receive Consumer Interaction Training (which should include methods of conflict resolution) in addition to the newsletter.
- Security personnel receive additional training on:
  - Conflict Resolution Training
  - Physical Training—how to control a person physically without hurting him/her
  - Training on how to manage a situation if it does occur

Human Resources

Prevention Responsibilities

- Report any problems to the ERT immediately.
- Answer employees' questions concerning the GEA Workplace Violence Policy.
- Assure that the GEA Workplace Violence Policy including zero tolerance of violence is enforced.
    - Report known incidents.
    - Encourage people to come forward with information (maintain confidentiality wherever possible).
    - Do not ignore the problem.
    - Document all incidents.
- Refer employees to EAP when helpful.
- Empathize with employee—understand the employee's feelings in a particular situation.

Incident Responsibilities

- Facilitate communication from ERT to top management.
- Provide information on employees involved in the situation.
- Provide any necessary back-up support (i.e., meeting rooms, snacks, tissues).

Post-Incident Responsibilities

- Obtain copies of the personnel records of victim(s) and person committing the violent act.
    - Organize/document any information from the record which may be relevant to the investigation.
- Notify and interact with the family of the victim(s).
- Deliver the employee's personal belongings to employee or his/her family.
- Prepare an accident/incident fact sheet.

Communications

Prevention Responsibilities

- Prepare and distribute news stories and other communications of the GEA Workplace Violence Policy and employee responsibilities concerning violence.
- Help disseminate information on the notification process—who should be called and when? Names and phone numbers

Incident Responsibilities

- Assure effective communication is maintained both within GEA and when dealing with outside sources.
- Notify all ERT members, responsible upper management, and corporate as soon as possible.
- Coordinate all communications with media.
  - [Name] is authorized spokesperson for the Company.
  - Get Legal's review of any official Company statements.
  - Provide current information.
  - Restrict media entry into the crisis area.

Post-Incident Responsibilities

- Provide input/feedback to the ERT on the handling of the situation.
- Provide any information which the employees should know.
  - When work will resume
  - Debriefing sessions scheduled

Medical/Counseling

Prevention Responsibilities

- Provide counseling to troubled employees through the Employee Assistance Program.
  - Publicize EAP; encourage its use.
- Assure a sufficient supply of emergency medical equipment is always on hand.

- Provide training on how to handle angry or disturbed employees who enter the facility.
- Help train employees on the warning signs.
- Identify outside resources (psychologist, psychiatrists, and therapists) who specialize in anger control or crisis management who will agree to provide evaluations, testing, and treatment for GEA employees.
- Consult with managers, employees, human resource representatives who report a potentially violent situation.
- If EAP believes a person/situation is potentially violent, these general findings regarding stability and risk must be reported to the ERT. EAP should make recommendations on how best to handle the situation.

Incident Responsibilities

- Treat any injured victims.
- If safe, attempt to calm the violent person.
- Make recommendations to the ERT.
- Assess the immediate needs of the affected employees.
- Call help if necessary (i.e., ambulance).

Post-Incident Responsibilities

- Conduct intervention as soon after the incident as possible.
- Assist affected employees in coping with the trauma.
- Advise management of what reactions they may expect from employees; develop a plan for coping with the incident.

Security

Prevention Responsibilities

- Increase security of GEA facilities as necessary.
- Receive and document all threat reports or violent incidents.
- Investigate threats; if serious, involve the full ERT.
- All violent incidents must be reported to the ERT and acted upon.
- Coordinate with local law enforcement.

- Gather building plans and maps of the facility.
- Assure security personnel receive conflict resolution training and physical training.

Incident Responsibilities

When contacted about a violent incident, security should obtain as much information as possible, including:

- the exact location of the incident.
- the number of victims.
- the nature of injuries, if any.
- the remaining hazards at the scene.
- the identity of the attacker(s), if known.

In addition:

- Call for help as necessary (i.e., police, ambulance).
- Notify full ERT of incident.
- Restrict entry into the area.
- Assist in evacuation of the area.
- Provide first aid, if appropriate.
- Work with the ERT.

Post-Incident Responsibilities

- Interview all witnesses and others having knowledge of the incident.
- Provide input/feedback to the ERT.
- Document the incident.

Prevention Responsibilities

- Report any problems to the ERT immediately.
- Answer employees' questions concerning the GEA Workplace Violence Policy.
- Assure that the GEA Workplace Violence Policy including zero tolerance of violence is enforced.
  - Report known incidents.
  - Encourage people to come forward with information (maintain confidentiality wherever possible).

- Do not ignore the problem.
- Document all incidents.
- Refer employees to EAP when helpful.
- Empathize with employee—understand the employee's feelings in a particular situation.

Incident Responsibilities

- Facilitate communication from ERT to top management.
- Provide information on employees involved in the situation.
- Provide any necessary back-up support (i.e., meeting rooms, snacks, tissues).

Post-Incident Responsibilities

- Obtain copies of the personnel records of victim(s) and person committing the violent act.
- Organize/document any information from the record which may be relevant to the investigation.
- Notify and interact with the family of the victim(s).
- Deliver the employee's personal belongings to employee or his/her family.
- Prepare an accident/incident fact sheet.

Affected Department: Operating Manager and Employees

Prevention Responsibilities

- Be alert for warning signs.
- Report any threats or potential for violence.
- Maintain good working conditions so workers are less likely to get frustrated and are more likely to come forward with information.

Incident Responsibilities

- Evacuate the area.
- Call Security, ERT member, or 911 (emergency numbers should be posted).
  - Provide as much information as possible (description of incident, any injuries, number of victims, remaining hazards, etc.).

- Provide first aid, if qualified.
- Stay with the victims if safe to do so (reassure them that help is coming).

Post-Incident Responsibilities

- Provide information to ERT and Security.
- Discuss employee reactions with EAP.
- Schedule a debriefing session or individual appointments with EAP.
- Don't expect things to be back to "normal" immediately.
- Talk with workers; discuss feelings.

Appendix 5c

THREAT INCIDENT REPORT

Company policy should require employees to report all threats or incidents of violent behavior which they observe or are informed about to the Designated Management Representative (DMR). The DMR should take the steps necessary to complete a threat incident report as quickly as possible, including private interview of the victims(s) and witness(es). The report will be used by the Threat Management Team to assess the safety of the workplace, and to decide upon a plan of action. The following facts should be included in the threat incident report:

- name of the threat-maker and his/her relationship to the company and to the recipient

- name(s) of the victims or potential victims

- when and where the incident occurred

- what happened immediately prior to the incident

- the specific language of the threat

- any physical conduct that would substantiate an intention to follow through on the threat

- how the threat-maker appeared (physically and emotionally)

- names of others who were directly involved and any actions they took

- how the incident ended

- names of witnesses

- what happened to the threat-maker after the incident

- what happened to the other employees directly involved after the incident

- names of any supervisory staff involved and how they responded

- what event(s) triggered the incident

- any history leading up to the incident

- the steps which have been taken to ensure that the threat will not be carried out

- suggestions for preventing workplace violence in the future

Elements of the threat incident report and any subsequent actions relating to the incident should be recorded in a tracking system for use by the DMR and the Threat Management Team. Such systems range from simple card files to commercially available relational databases. The tracking system as well as all investigative files, should be kept secure and maintained separately from other records.

References

Adler, F., G.O.W. Mueller & W.S. Laufer (1995). *Criminology: The Shorter Version, Second Edition*. New York, NY: McGraw-Hill, Inc.

"A New Worry: Going to Work Can Be Murder" (1993, February 25). *The New York Times*, B1.

Askari, E. (1991, November 15). "Curiosity Shock, Cynicism at Scene: Reactions Vary Among Residents and Visitors." *Detroit Free Press*, 14A.

Baker, S.P., J.S. Samkoff, R.S. Fisher & C.B. Vanburen (1982). "Fatal Occupational Injuries." *Journal of the American Medical Association*, 248:692-697.

Bell, C.A. (1991). "Female Homicides in United States Workplaces, 1980-1985." *American Journal of Public Health*, 81(6):729-732.

Bell, C.A., N.A. Stout, T.R. Bender, C.S. Conroy, W.E. Crouse & J.R. Myers (1990). "Fatal Occupational Injuries in the United States, 1980 through 1985." *Journal of the American Medical Association*, 263(22):3047-3050.

Bensimon, H.F. (1994, January). "Violence in the Workplace." *Training and Development*, 27-32.

Berelson, B. (1952). "Content Analysis." In L. Gardner (ed.) *Handbook of Social Psychology, Theory and Method*, (1):488-522.

Buzawa, E.G. & C.G. Buzawa (1990). *Domestic Violence: The Criminal Justice Response*. Studies in Crime, Law and Justice, Volume 6. Newbury Park, CA: Sage Publications, Inc.

Cahill, J. (1990, November). "Postal Workers on the Edge: A Study of Mail Handler Job Stress." *International Publication*. Glassboro, NJ: Glassboro State College.

189

Carmel, H. & M. Hunter (1990). "Compliance with Training in Managing Assaultive Behavior and Injuries from In-Patient Violence." *Hospital Community Psychiatry*, 41(5):558-560.

Centers for Disease Control (1992). *Homicide in U.S. Workplaces: A Strategy for Prevention and Research*. Morgantown, WV: Division of Safety Research, National Institute for Occupational Safety and Health.

Center for Disease Control and Prevention (1989). *National Traumatic Occupational Fatalities: 1980-1985*. Atlanta, GA: U.S. Department of Health and Human Services, Public Health Service.

Cheatwood, D. & K.J. Block (1990). "Youth and Homicide: An Investigation of the Age Factor in Criminal Homicide." *Justice Quarterly*, 7(2):265-292.

Cheng, M.M. & R. Polner (1995, December 20). "Merchant's Wife, Four Others Slain Over Sneakers." *The Paducah Sun*, 2A.

Cohen, L.E. & M. Felson (1993). "A Routine Activity Approach." In F.P. Williams III & M.D. McShane (eds.) *Criminology Theory: Selected Classic Readings*, pp. 267-275. Cincinnati, OH: Anderson Publishing Co.

Cohen, L.E. & M. Felson (1979). "Social Change and Crime Rate Trends: A Routine Activity Approach." *American Sociological Review*, 44(August):588-608.

Corder, B.F., B.C. Ball, T.M. Haizlip, R. Rollins & R. Beaumont (1976). "Adolescent Parricide: A Comparison with Other Adolescent Murder." *American Journal of Psychiatry*, 133(8):957-961.

D'Addario, F. (1995). *The Manager's Violence Survival Guide*. Chapel Hill, NC: Crime Prevention Association.

D'Addario, F. (1990, June). "The Cooperative Fight Against Violent Crime." *Security Management*, 57-60.

Daly, M. & M. Wilson (1988). *Homicide*. New York, NY: Aldine-De Gruyter.

Davis, H. (1987). "Workplace Homicides in Texas Males." *American Journal of Public Health*, 77(10):1290-1293.

Davis, H., P.S. Honchar & L. Suarez (1987). "Fatal Occupational Injuries of Women, Texas 1975-1984." *American Journal of Public Health*, 77:1524-1527.

Department of Industrial Relations (1994, August). In *CAL/OSHA Guidelines for Workplace Security, California Health and Safety Code: 1257.7 and 1257.8*, p. 21. San Francisco, CA: Division of Occupational Safety and Health.

Dietz, P.E. & S.P. Baker (1987). "Murder at Work." *American Journal of Public Health*, 77(10):1273-1274.

Discipline Practices in the U.S. Postal Services: Hearing Before the Subcommittee on Census, Statistics, Postal Personnel; and Postal Operations and Services, House of Representatives, 105th Cong. (1994, August 5) (testimony of Marvin Runyon).

Ebring, L. (1980, June). *News Media Monitoring and Modeling Public Opinion Dynamics*, p. 6. Chicago, IL: University of Chicago.

Fagan, J. (1989). "Cessation of Family Violence: Deterrence and Dissuasion." In L. Ohlin & M. Tonry (eds.) *Crime and Justice: A Review of Research*, Volume 11, pp. 377-426. Chicago, IL: University of Chicago Press.

Felson, R.B. & S.F. Messner (1996). "To Kill or Not to Kill? Lethal Outcomes in Injurious Attacks." *Criminology*, 34(4):519-545.

Fenby, J. (1986). *The International News Services: A Twentieth Century Fund Report*. New York, NY: Schocken Books.

Fisher, R.W. (1991). *Violence in the Workplace: Crisis Intervention at the Royal Oak Post Office: A Case Study.* United States Postal Service.

Florida Office of Attorney General Robert A. Butterworth (1991, January). *Study of Safety and Security Requirement for At-Risk Businesses*. State of Florida.

Frisaro, F.R. (1996, February 10). "Ex-Worker on Florida Beach Detail Fatally Shoots 5, Self." *The Paducah Sun*, 2A.

Gelles, R.J. (1987). *Family Violence*. Sage Library of Social Research, Volume 84, Newbury Park, CA: Sage Publications, Inc.

Gottfredson, M.R. & T. Hirschi (1990). *A General Theory of Crime*. Stanford, CA: Stanford University Press.

Guidelines for Preventing Workplace Violence for Health Care and Social Service Workers (1996). U.S. Department of Labor Occupational Safety and Health Administration: OSHA 3148.

Hales, T., P. Seligman, S. Newman & C. Timbrook (1988). "Occupational Injuries Due to Violence." *Journal of Occupational Medicine*, 30(6):483-487.

Harwood, D. (1927). *Getting and Writing News*. New York, NY: George H. Doran Company.

Heide, K.M. (1995). *Why Kids Kill Parents: Child Abuse and Adolescent Homicide*. Thousand Oaks, CA: Sage Publications, Inc.

Hickey, E.W. (1991). *Serial Murderers and Their Victims*, pp. 203-217. Belmont, CA: Wadsworth Publishing Co.

Indiana Department of Labor (1991, March). Serious Safety Order No. 1 (Amended).

"A Response to Occupational Violent Crime." Indianapolis, IN: Occupational Safety and Health Administration. As cited in J. Thomas (1992, June). *Risk Control*, 27-31.

Jeffery, C.R. (1977). *Crime Prevention Through Environment Design*. Beverly Hills, CA: Sage Publications, Inc.

Jenkins, E.L., L. Lagne & S. Kisher (1992). "Homicide in the Workplace: The U.S. Experience, 1980-1988." *AAOHN Journal*, 40(5):215-218.

Kadaba, L. (1993, December 7). "Violence Increases in the Workplace." *The Philadelphia Inquirer*, F1.

Kaufer, S. (1993). *After the Crisis: Dealing with the Media*. Chicago, IL: Workplace Violence Research Institute, 9-49 to 9-56.

Kaufer, S. (1992). "Violence in the Workplace Can Be Prevented." In *Security Topics*, 3. Palm Springs, CA: Inter/Action Associates.

Kinney, J.A. & D.L. Johnson (1993). *Breaking Point: The Workplace Violence Epidemic and What to Do About It*. Chicago, IL: National Safe Workplace Institute.

Kraus, J.F. (1987). "Homicide While at Work: Persons, Industries, and Occupations at High Risk." *American Journal of Public Health*, 77(10):1285-1289.

Larson, E. (1994, October 13). "Trigger Happy a False Crisis: How Workplace Violence Became a Hot Issue." *The Wall Street Journal*, A1.

Leader, S.H. (1990). *Violence and Sabotage by Disgruntled Employees,* Second Draft. Washington, DC: Technical Report prepared for the U.S. Department of Energy.

Levin, J. & J.A. Fox (1985). *Mass Murder: America's Growing Menace*. New York, NY: Plenum.

Livingston, J. (1996). *Crime & Criminology*, Second Edition. Upper Saddle River, NJ: Prentice Hall.

Losey, J.F. (1994, February). "Managing in a Era of Workplace Violence." *Managing Office Technology*, 27-28.

MacDougall, A.K. (1968, January 18). "Grinding It Out: AP, UPI Fight Fiercely for Front-Page Space As They Cover the World." *Wall Street Journal*, 1.

Maguire, K. & A. Pastore (1995). *Sourcebook of Criminal Justice Statistics 1994*. Washington, DC: U.S. Government Printing Office.

Maguire, K., A. Pastore & T. Flanagan (1993). *Sourcebook of Criminal Justice Statistics 1992*. Washington, DC: U.S. Government Printing Office.

Marshall, K. & B. Rossman (1989). *Designing Qualitative Research*. Newbury Park, CA: Sage Publications, Inc.

Mills, C.W. (1972). "Mass Media and Public Opinion." In A. Caswty (ed.) *Mass Media and Mass Man*, Second Edition, pp. 184-190. Washington, DC: Holt, Rinehart and Winston.

"Model for Combating Violence in the Workplace" (1993). *Security Journal.* 4(2):16.

Monahan, J. (1994, January). "The Causes of Violence." *FBI Law Enforcement Bulletin*, 11-15.

National Committee for Injury Prevention and Control (1989). *Injury Prevention: Meeting the Challenge*. New York, NY: Oxford University Press.

National Crime Prevention Institute (1987). *Understanding Crime Prevention.* Stoneham, MA: Butterworth Publishers.

National Safe Workplace Institute (1988). *Safer Work: Job Safety and Health Challenges for the Next President and Congress.* Chicago, IL: NSWI.

Nelsen, C., J. Corzine & L. Huff-Corzine (1994). "The Violent West Reexamined: A Research Note on Regional Homicide Rates." *Criminology,* 32(1):149-161.

NIOSH (1993). *Fatal Injuries to Workers in the United States, 1980-1989: A Decade of Surveillance: National Profile.* Cincinnati, OH: U.S. Department of Health and Human Services, Public Health Service, Center for Disease Control and Prevention, National Institute for Occupational Safety and Health, DHHS (NIOSH), 93-108.

NIOSH (1993, September). *Preventing Homicide in the Workplace.* Cincinnati, OH: U.S. Department of Health and Human Services, Public Health Service, Center for Disease Control and Prevention, National Institute for Occupational Safety and Health, DHHS (NIOSH), 93-109.

Nisbett, R. (1993). "Violence and U.S. Regional Culture." *American Psychologist,* 48:441-449.

Northwestern National Life Insurance Company (1993, October). *Fear and Violence in the Workplace: An In-House Survey.* Chicago, IL.

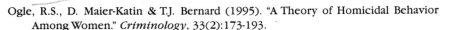

O'Boyle, T.F. (1992). "Disgruntled Workers Intent on Revenge Increasingly Harm Colleagues and Bosses." *Wall Street Journal,* B1, B10.

Ogle, R.S., D. Maier-Katin & T.J. Bernard (1995). "A Theory of Homicidal Behavior Among Women." *Criminology,* 33(2):173-193.

Ohlin, L. & M. Tonry (1989a). "Family Violence in Perspective." In L. Ohlin & M. Tonry (eds.) *Crime and Justice: A Review of Research,* Volume 11, pp. 1-18. Chicago, IL: University of Chicago Press.

Ohlin, L. & M. Tonry (eds.) (1989b). *Crime and Justice: A Review of Research,* Volume 11. Chicago, IL: University of Chicago Press.

"Opryland Trio Shot at Employee Hotel" (1995, May 19). *The Tennessean,* A1.

Pagelow, M.D. (1989). "The Incidence and Prevalence of Criminal Abuse of Other Family Members." In L. Ohlin & M. Tonry (eds.) *Crime and Justice: A Review of Research,* Volume 11, pp. 263-314. Chicago, IL: University of Chicago Press.

"Postal Study Aims to Spot Violence-Prone Workers" (1993, July 2). *The New York Times,* A19.

Reiss, A. & J. Roth (eds.) (1993). *Understanding and Preventing Violence.* Washington, DC: National Academy Press.

Rivers, William L. (1964). *The Mass Media: Reporting—Writing—Editing.* New York, NY: Harper and Row.

Robinson, M.J. & M.A. Sheehan (1983). *Over the Wire and on TV: CBS and UPI in Campaign '80*. New York, NY: Russell Sage Foundation.

Roth, J.A. (1994, February). "Understanding and Preventing Violence." *NIJ Research in Brief*. Washington, DC: U.S. Department of Justice.

Seger, K.A. (1993). "Violence in the Workplace: An Assessment of the Problem Based on Responses from 32 Large Corporations." *Security Journal*, 4(3):139-149.

Seger, K.A. (1992). *An Assessment of Available Instruments for Psychological Evaluations*. Oak Ridge, TN: Oak Ridge Institute for Science and Education, Medical Sciences Division. Center for Human Reliability Studies.

Shaw, D. (1969). "Surveillance vs. Constraint: Press Coverage of a Social Issue." *Journalism Quarterly*, 56(Winter):707-712.

Sigler, R.T. (1989). *Domestic Violence in Context: An Assessment of Community Attitudes*. Lexington, MA: Lexington Books.

Solomon, J. & P. King (1993, July 19). "Waging War in the Workplace." *Newsweek*, 30-34.

Southerland, M.D. & P. Collins (1994). "Workplace Violence: A 'Recent Case' Analysis." *Journal of Security Administration*, 17(2):1-10.

"Teasing of Heavy Officer May Have Led to Shooting" (1997, January 19). *The Paducah Sun*, 2A.

Thomas, J.L. (1992). "Occupational Violent Crime: Research on an Emerging Issue." *Journal of Safety Research*, 23(2):55-62.

Thomas, J.L. (1992, June). "A Response to Occupational Violent Crime." *Risk Control*, 27-31.

U.S. Congress (1990, September). "The Use of Integrity Tests for Pre-Employment Screening: OTA-SET-422." Washington, DC: U.S. Government Printing Office. Office of Technology Assessment.

U.S. Department of Justice, Federal Bureau of Investigation (1996). *Crime in the United States, 1995*. Washington, DC: U.S. Government Printing Office.

U.S. Department of Justice, Federal Bureau of Investigation (1995). *Crime in the United States, 1994*. Washington, DC: U.S. Government Printing Office.

U.S. Department of Labor (1994, February). "Workplace Homicides in 1992." *Compensation and Working Conditions*. Washington, DC: Bureau of Labor Statistics.

U.S. House of Representatives (1989, May 23 & June 7). "Discipline Practices in the U.S. Postal Services: Subcommittee on Postal Personnel and Modernization." Washington, DC.

Walton, J.B. (1995). *Violence in the Workplace: The Employer's Guide to Identifying and Handling the Potentially Violent Employee*. New York, NY: McGraw-Hill, College Custom Series Publications.

Weber, R.P. (1990). *Basic Content Analysis*, Second Edition. Newbury Park, CA: Sage Publications, Inc.

What You Should Know About Coping with Threats and Violence in the Federal Workplace. [Electronic data file] (Updated October 1995). Washington, DC: U.S. General Services Administration, Public Building Service.

Wilson, M.I. & M. Daly (1992). "Who Kills Whom in Spouse Killings? On the Exceptional Sex Ratio of Spousal Homicides in the United States." *Criminology,* 30(2):189-215.

Wyman, T.P. (1995, October 21). "Man Kills Wife, Self in Shooting at Bank." *The Paducah Sun,* 2A.

Index

warning signs pg.169